T0355014

Be Wild,

Be Crazy,

Be You!

Be Wild,

OPEN YOUR HEART AND MIND.

Be Crazy,

FEEL THE CONFIDENCE.

Be You!

JEAN MACDONALD

ARCHWAY
PUBLISHING

Archway Publishing books may be ordered through booksellers or by contacting:

Archway Publishing
1663 Liberty Drive
Bloomington, IN 47403
www.archwaypublishing.com
844-669-3957

Interior Image Credit: Jean MacDonald

ISBN: 978-1-6657-6452-0 (sc)
ISBN: 978-1-6657-6454-4 (hc)
ISBN: 978-1-6657-6453-7 (e)

Library of Congress Control Number: 2024917300

Print information available on the last page.

Archway Publishing rev. date: 10/11/2024

CONTENTS

Preface.. xi

Chapter 1 The Beginning..1
Chapter 2 Change Your Mind 13
Chapter 3 The Journey Continues.................................24
Chapter 4 Developing Confidence 42
Chapter 5 Finding the Fire 53
Chapter 6 Building Our Children's Confidence.............72
Chapter 7 The Power of Self-Esteem 78
Chapter 8 Feel the Love 90
Chapter 9 Change..103
Chapter 10 Next Steps.. 111

Contributors 117
Acknowledgments..125
About the Author..129

Also by Jean Macdonald

Get Up, Get Dressed, Get Out the Door (Ace Publishing 2012)
Finding the Fortune (Ace Publishing 2017)

To the women who have shaped, guided, and inspired me.

This book is for the brave souls who dare to leap, even when the stones are slippery and the path uncertain.

To my mother and father, who showed me what true strength looks like. To my friends and mentors who believed in me when I couldn't believe in myself.

My greatest sources of joy and inspiration are my husband, children, and grandchildren. Your boundless curiosity and resilience remind me daily of the power of confidence and love.

And to every woman seeking her own confidence, may you find the courage to act and discover the strength within.

With gratitude and love,

Jean MacDonald

You're someone who knows her own heart …
who's not afraid to follow where it leads.
—Anonymous

PREFACE

My life has been a series of milestones, like stepping stones in a brook. I have jumped from rock to rock—some large, where I land solidly in the middle; others small, requiring careful balance to stay in place. Some stones are slimy and covered with moss, making them treacherous and sometimes disastrous to jump on. I have jumped on more than I would like to admit, falling, losing my balance, scraping my knees, getting up, and eventually moving on. Sound easy? Well, I would be lying if I said it was.

This book is a collection of stories and milestones from my life, encompassing moments of lack of confidence, failure, and success. I have also woven in stories of remarkable women I have met along the way.

I asked them to consider five questions and choose the one that resonated with them the most:

- What does confidence mean to you?
- Who is a role model for you in showing confidence?
- Can you share how confidence has helped you overcome obstacles or pushed you beyond what you thought you could do?
- What daily practices or readings do you engage in to grow your confidence?
- What advice would you give a younger woman seeking greater confidence?

Confidence, by definition, is the belief that one can rely on someone or something; it's a firm trust. Having self-confidence means having faith in oneself.

What is confidence? How do we acquire it? Are we born with it, or is it something we learn through life's challenges? Some of the most harrowing experiences can build confidence, sometimes bordering on cockiness. Yet I have also witnessed individuals who struggle through challenging times without recovery, becoming introverted and stuck in the drama.

So what does it take to build our confidence? How do we motivate ourselves to gain confidence? Being confident means knowing you can handle the emotional outcomes of life's challenges.

Start by acknowledging every emotion, including the difficult ones, rather than avoiding them. Speaking up for yourself, limiting self-criticism, and employing other strategies can help build emotional strength and confidence.

I had pondered writing this book for a long time. Finally, putting it into print required great courage and confidence. What was holding me back? Why was I feeling stuck? I needed to break out of my bubble, understand my purpose, and let my best self shine.

Allow these tips and stories to inspire you to break free from any slump, try new things, discover your calling, aim higher, and be the best version of yourself.

Remember: Courage + Action = Confidence.

CHAPTER 1

The Beginning

A Heartfelt Journey: From Adopted to Empowered

On December 10, 1950, a baby girl was born at Somerset Hospital in Somerville, New Jersey. There were no balloons, flowers, hugs, or celebrations. The young woman who had this beautiful little girl was only sixteen. This new baby girl was being put up for adoption. What a traumatic and difficult decision for the family, but a wise one, considering the mother's young age. The baby would leave the hospital and stay at the Children's Home Society in Trenton, New Jersey, until she would be united with a new adopting family.

Let me set the stage for this new baby and her new adoptive parents. William and Marie Carter were married on October 7, 1945. They lived in Trenton, New Jersey. Over the next few years, they tried to have a baby but were unsuccessful. There were two miscarriages and one painful stillbirth. They were heartbroken and felt they would never have a child. Marie's mother suggested they adopt a baby. Back in the 1950s, this was highly unusual. Other members of the adopting family rarely accepted adoptees as part of their extended family. In addition, the adoption process was both expensive and time-consuming. Despite the obstacles, the Carters knew they could offer a child a loving home. After filling out reams of paper and having several interviews, the couple was told that a baby was available. The adoption took place on May 5, 1951. The baby girl was delivered to their home.

The celebration for them was tears of joy. I found, years later, a speech my father prepared, addressing adoption. He said, "Jean adopted us and made our house a home." Many did not accept my mom and dad adopting a young child. My aunt, father's sister, and great-aunt Elsie were never really accepting of me, but I did not realize this until many years later.

When I was five, we moved to Bordentown, New Jersey. My parents built a new home in the suburbs so my father could be close to McGuire Air Force Base. He worked for MAC (Military Airlift Command) as a civilian contractor. His job involved coordinating the movement of high-value cargo, such as aircraft and equipment parts, and transporting troops to and from combat zones.

I started kindergarten in the fall and was excited to meet new friends in a new area, but I had no idea how cruel children could be. I was often teased and made fun of as a girl in grammar school. I remember going to school one day, feeling so happy after celebrating my adoptive birthday. Mom made a special cake with angel candles. My dad, grandmother, and grandfather were there, and we sang and laughed. When I mentioned this in class at school, they teased me. I remember going home feeling ashamed and sad, asking my mom, "Why are they so mean to me?" She said they were jealous that they had not been chosen. She would pat me on the head, hug me, and say, "Who loves you?" I would answer, "You love me." Mom would reply, "You are right, and that is all that matters."

Years passed, and I was at my twentieth high school reunion. One of the girls from class came over to me and introduced herself, saying, "I need to apologize."

At first, I wasn't sure what she meant, but she went on to tell me that she was one of those who had picked on me and made fun of me for being adopted. She then went on to say that she had adopted two children, unable to have any of her own. She said it was the most joyous time when these children came into her life. "Please forgive me," she said. I was taken aback but accepted her apology graciously and thanked her for her honesty.

What an enormously positive change that adoption has become so prevalent and accepted today! I have met so many who have been adopted or who have adopted children.

Why is this story so important? Because of the circumstances of my early life, my self-confidence could have plummeted and stayed there, but instead, I began to build up my self-assurance as a young girl. Partly, this came about because I had phenomenal parents. My mother was a gracious, extraordinary woman who was always dressed beautifully from head to toe. She taught me how to be a classy, warm, genuine woman. She would say, "If you don't ask, you don't get! So ask, Jean, and be assertive. Not everyone will give you the decision you want, but you will never know if you don't ask."

Who believed in you and gave you the confidence to move through difficult situations, and how did this affect your confidence?

***

Seeds of Confidence: Growing a Business with Dad's Tomatoes

If you don't ask, you don't get!
—**Marie Carter**

It's been said that nothing happens until somebody sells something. While this may be true, the more profound truth is that building relationships reaps the bigger reward—not just a single sale but ongoing sales to customers who have come to know and trust you.

My sales journey began one hot August day when I was twelve. My family lived in an extensive housing development with more than eighty homes, so there were plenty of kids to hang out with. We'd get together beneath one of the big shade trees and have fun dreaming up things to do. We all liked the idea of getting more money, and one day, we decided that opening lemonade stands would be an excellent way to raise some. We were sure all the neighbors would happily pay us for a nice, cold drink on a warm summer day. We'd have fun and make money at the same time.

Fired up, I raced home to tell my mom about our plan. Dad came in the door, and we walked into the house together. I chattered excitedly about my new business venture, and he was pleased that I wanted to become a young entrepreneur. We found Mom in the kitchen, even busier than usual with the annual tomato-canning ritual. My father was renowned in the neighborhood for his big, juicy beefsteak tomatoes (he'd even won awards for size, color, and taste), and Mom was at the countertop, surrounded by a sea of ripe red tomatoes ready to be packed in large, glass mason jars.

She listened as Dad and I sat at the table and discussed my business plan. After a few moments, he nodded thoughtfully and said, "I want you to sit here for a few minutes and think about this project. You know the other kids will be doing the same thing, and you'll all try to sell the same product, which will surely cut your sales. Can you think of another approach? A different idea?"

He could tell I wasn't quite getting his drift, so he made a suggestion. "Sit here and look around you for a few minutes. See if you can come up with something." With that, he got up from his chair and told me he'd be back soon to find out what I had come up with.

I did as he said, sitting quietly at the table and looking around as Mom busied herself with the canning. Then it struck me—I could sell Dad's tomatoes! We always had an overabundance, so many that we'd have to give them away. Why not sell them instead? People constantly asked for them and would happily pay for something that delicious.

It sounded good, but I didn't know where to start. I was not sure they would buy anything from a twelve-year-old. Was I ready for this new venture? Would all the other kids laugh at me since they were all setting up lemonade stands?

But then I remembered my mom always saying, "If you don't ask, you don't get, Jean, so go ahead and ask."

When Dad returned to the kitchen, I was fired up, a little hesitant, but ready to begin my entrepreneurial career. He was smart; he knew that if he left me alone to think of a solution, I would take ownership of the idea and run with it. Once that happened, he supported me all the way. We prepared by giving my red wagon a new coat of paint to deliver my product and bought a receipt book and a bag to hold my money. That summer's business venture was a tremendous success. Everyone loved Dad's tomatoes. I even expanded my offerings to include his cucumbers and carrots.

Dad asked me what I needed to do next at the end of the season. Not knowing the answer, I asked for his advice. He explained that it was time to prepare for the upcoming season, gather the neighbors' names and addresses, and stay in touch with them. He even suggested that I send them handwritten notes thanking them for their business and letting them know I would be back next year.

That summer, my dad taught me a valuable lesson about making people feel important and following up, letting them know I would return to do business with them again.

The confidence it gave me was the fabric to build my career.

Reflect on a childhood experience or lesson that has shaped your approach to challenges and opportunities. How can you leverage those early lessons in your current endeavors?

***

Emma, my granddaughter, wrote and presented this speech. She was twelve at the time. Emma offered this speech at the Optimist Club Contest. She won the school and area contest and went on to deliver and compete in the state competition. We are so proud that she finished fourth in the contest, competing against high school students. She was the youngest competitor. Her speech fits this book very well. Optimist International's mission is to bring out the best in youth, community, and ourselves.

How Does One Find Optimism?
Emma Schoch

Discovering optimism is finding positivity and light within yourself.

The word "discovering" means finding or uncovering something, such as something you didn't know you had, like a family heirloom, or finding out who you are. The phrase "optimism within me" means finding the cheerful burst of happiness inside you. You could find optimism in challenging times or when another family member or friend struggles. There are many ways that people can discover optimism within themselves, even during a very low or painful time in their lives.

Many people have found optimism within themselves, just like Denzel Washington, Tim Tebow, and me. Denzel's future was written on paper by a woman in his mother's beauty parlor. Tim Tebow created the Tim Tebow Foundation and helped hundreds of children with disabilities who were abused or had traumatic experiences. Lastly, I found optimism within myself by going through many obstacles and struggles in my life.

Denzel Washington once said, "I say luck is when an opportunity comes along, and you're prepared for it." Before all his fame and success, Denzel was going to flunk out of school, and he had a hard time with his grades and staying focused at Fordham University. Denzel went to his mother's beauty parlor one day, and this woman was staring at him. He walked over to the woman, and she said, "I have a prophecy." She wrote it on paper and handed it to him. It said, "Boy, you will travel the world and speak to millions." A few years later, he began a successful acting career, and through that, he started to travel worldwide, speaking to colleges and students.

He talked about God and the great wonders he did and how hard work and being optimistic will get you far in life. He discovered the optimism within him because a woman believed in him and prophesied his future, and with help from God, Denzel is now living in it.

Tim Tebow was a famous football player who was very devoted to Christ. He was known for writing bible verses on his black eye every time he played. He used his money to create the Tim Tebow Foundation (TTF) to help children whose parents abused them, children with disabilities, and children undergoing traumatic experiences.

As the foundation grew, an event called "Night to Shine" began. The "Night to Shine" is for all the children at the foundation to get dressed up, walk the red carpet, and party all night long. Tim Tebow said, "We must humble ourselves, and you do that by serving others." By helping all those children, Tim Tebow discovered optimism within him, and as he helped others, they found it in themselves.

Lastly, I had difficulty deciding whether to keep this person or pick someone else. I decided I would keep this person, and that person is myself. I have had a roller coaster of emotions and challenges throughout my life. I always had difficulty believing in myself and knowing I could do anything if I put my mind to it. In the past years, I have accomplished many things; through these experiences, I have grown stronger in believing in myself. A quote from the Optimist Creed states, "To forget the mistakes of the past and press on to the greater achievements of the future."

I have always held on to my little mistakes and forgotten that I can't control them, and this quote is an excellent example of my life. If I get just one little error on a test, I keep thinking about that little mistake instead of saying, "How am I going to make this better?" Over the years, I have been building up confidence, courage, and trust in myself, and those experiences have made me the person I am today.

Earlier, I asked, how does one find optimism within themselves?

Sometimes, it is right before you or a few steps ahead. Anyone at any age can discover optimism within themselves. We all have difficulties, but the downs make us stronger. Every day, strive to be the best you can be.

Every day, strive to put yourself out there and take a chance.

Every day, strive to be who you are, who God made you to be. The Optimist Creed says, "to be so strong that nothing can disturb your peace of mind." So today, tomorrow, and every day, try to find that optimism so that nothing, not even a little setback, can disturb your peace of mind.

My twelve-year-old granddaughter and her speech taught me (or reminded me) to look at things with a new perspective.

***

A Journey from Setbacks to Self-Discovery

I realized I could sell at an early age, but getting the break I needed would take several years. Why was that? My mother's encouragement and my father's guidance taught me valuable lessons. They taught me how to treat people with kindness, be of service to others, and always do what I promised. These lessons have given me the confidence to be the woman I am today. Sounds easy.

I enjoyed doing things my way and not listening to my peers, which caused me a lot of pain and setbacks over the years. I could have gone much further and faster if I had taken the advice of others.

That's the problem with confidence. Sometimes too much confidence can make us cocky. Being a know-it-all when I lacked maturity cost me dearly. I always had to be in charge, but was I?

Let me step back. When I was eighteen, after attending college at the University of Tampa in Florida for one year, I was a poor student and didn't know what I wanted. I met my then-to-be husband during my first year of college. He was a junior, and we decided to get married. We married that year, but I did not return to college and needed a job. We were living in Tampa, and I found this opportunity to work for an insurance agency as gal Friday. I did everything from making coffee to running errands and answering phones. It was 1969, and this was the perfect job for someone with no skills but a lot of ambition. I knew that if I could work hard, someday I could sell insurance and make real money. My then-husband graduated from college, and in 1970, we moved back to New Jersey.

We struggled with many things that happened along the way, including the birth of our son. Our marriage was failing. We had moved from Florida to New Jersey, where we were both from. We spent time living with his parents—a big mistake. We ended up getting divorced in 1974.

I was in challenging circumstances. My ex-husband's parents were unhappy with the decision and with me. My mom was battling cancer, which added to the emotional turmoil. Yet, amid the chaos, a flicker of determination remained.

Securing a junior underwriter role at a national insurance company provided stability, yet my aspirations lay in commercial insurance sales. The stumbling block was that very few women sold commercial insurance, but I was determined to get my agent license and break into this part of the business.

My boss at this insurance company came to the underwriting team one afternoon and informed us that anyone interested in a marketing job for the company should go to his office after work the next day. I was so excited. I knew this could be the stepping stone I needed to move into commercial insurance eventually.

It turned out that I was the only one interested, and the next day, I went to his office after everyone had left. To my astonishment, he proceeded to drop his pants when I closed the door to his office. I was scared, angry, and demoralized. As he stood there with his pants lying on the ground, I stepped back and said, "What do you want me to do with that thing?"

I turned around, slammed the door, picked up the things from my desk, and never returned to this company.

Have the confidence to walk away.

I cried all the way home. I had no job. I had a two-year-old, and I felt more alone than ever. I could not tell anyone. Who would believe me? I did not want to share it with my parents. My mom was so sick, and Dad had too many things on his plate to deal with this one. I was not attacked or raped, but I felt humiliated and distraught. Now what?

Alone and uncertain, I embarked on a journey of self-renewal. Sharing my ordeal was daunting yet necessary for my healing. Refusing to succumb to despair, I threw myself into networking and job hunting, determined to reclaim my narrative.

Life's trials can either paralyze or empower us. I chose the latter. Armed with courage and propelled by action, I navigated the tumultuous waters, emerging more assertive and more resilient. My formula for success? Courage + Action = Confidence.

CHAPTER 2

Change Your Mind

Change your mind to change your life.
—**Anonymous**

Diamonds in Disguise: Reinvention and Success

Change is essential to break free from being unstuck and move forward. Are you open to embracing change? The adage goes, if you keep doing the same things, you will get the same results. Embracing change can be invigorating and lead to entirely new horizons.

I made excuses, knowing that this wasn't the real me. After departing from the insurance company, fate introduced me to a man who owned a commercial insurance agency. It's true what they say—when one door closes, another opens.

I vividly recall my beginnings at the insurance agency in New Jersey. I was young, full of piss and vinegar (as my mother would put it), and eager to dive into sales. I felt unstoppable (or so I thought).

Back in the seventies, there were few women in the commercial insurance business, and I had worked various roles from administrative assistant to receptionist, junior underwriter, and customer service representative. Finally, I landed a position at an agency that allowed me to obtain my license to sell property and casualty insurance.

I was ecstatic, thinking I was on the path to sales success. However, my boss had different plans. He wanted me to handle existing accounts. It was like starting over. Unhappy with the situation, I began searching for a new job. At agency after agency, I faced rejection and failure.

But diamonds are waiting for each of us.

Finally, I received a lead about a local agency looking for new sales associates. I met with the owner, who offered me a job at $300 a week for three months, followed by a straight commission. The prospect of working on commission alone terrified me. He said, "It's simple, and most people miss it. There are two keys to success."

He instructed me to grab a pen and paper and take notes. First, he said, "All you need to do is pick up the diamonds lying on the ground." Initially puzzled, I soon realized he was onto something, owning a multimillion-dollar agency.

I listened intently, jotting down his wisdom. He explained that many overlook the diamonds—the relationships we cultivate, our attitude, and the care we invest in follow-up. These, he emphasized, are the first key to success. It takes time to learn, but the credibility and integrity we build are priceless.

Now, you might be wondering about the second key to success. According to him, it stems from our actions and how we assist others. When we work intelligently and earn our stripes, the second key is paying it forward, mentoring others, and aiding in their growth.

Initially, his words seemed abstract, but it all clicked as I worked alongside him, observing how he valued customer care and solid relationships. He was a master at fostering connections and boosting others' confidence.

His words resonated deeply with me, underscoring the importance of cultivating strong business relationships. Experience taught me that everyone wears an invisible sign that reads, "Make me feel important."

I engaged with my customers by showing respect, actively listening, seeking referrals, and uncovering hidden opportunities in everything I did.

I often see people solely chasing business without regard for others, missing opportunities for genuine connections and disregarding needs.

As I mentioned, when you help and reach out to others, it will return tenfold.

The real lesson from all this was the resilience my boss instilled in me. Failing is not a setback but an opportunity to learn and grow, fostering the confidence needed for improvement.

Remember, diamonds are all around us, waiting to be discovered. All it takes is the willingness to bend down and pick them up.

What diamonds are on the ground waiting for you to pick them up?

***

Good things happen when you refuse to quit …

Joanne and I first met in 1983, when a mutual travel agent introduced us. Since then, we have weathered life's difficulties together, finding solace in laughter and offering each other unwavering support. Regardless of one's religious or spiritual convictions, the author's narrative provides profound insight into how faith can instill the courage to navigate life's challenges with resilience and confidence.

Trusting the Journey:
A Story of Faith and Endurance
Joanne F. Cunneen

We talk a lot about finding the confidence within, but sometimes our greatest strength comes when our confidence is based on something outside ourselves.

I do not know why or how it happened, but I learned as a child that I was not alone. Children have fantasies, and I did too. But it was more than a fantasy—as experience would later reveal.

I sensed that God was with me, or more precisely, given my Christian upbringing, that Jesus was my companion. It was not the mystical Jesus that I heard preached about in religious education. It was always the human Jesus who was at my side. Never the scolding, judgmental Jesus but the Jesus who was a friend, affirming and strengthening me, a faithful companion. Quite a gift for a child, this faith—indeed, not a result of my doing, just something given, a grace.

I do not know why this faith—if that is what you want to call it—remained so much a part of me, even into adulthood. But if there is some divine providence, one could make the case that it was an essential gift for me, given how my life has progressed. At thirteen years of age, I was diagnosed as a person with type 1 diabetes and told that my life would not be a long one. It was a reasonable diagnosis at the time, for the available treatment was indeed primitive by today's standards. I took a shot of insulin in the morning, even though no one could tell my blood glucose level. This treatment allowed the disease to work its damage on my body slowly but measurably over time. I needed a companion to accompany me on this journey, which I knew was to end not abruptly but with many signposts pointing to the unavoidable and tragic culmination.

As an adult, I had ways of invoking the grace that had carried me through my early childhood. I embraced strength and courage, knowing that the virtues they pointed to were not self-generated but presented to me from another source. And I latched onto the words of the psalm—I do not even remember when they first came to me—"Lord, I place my trust in you."

It was later in life when the disease worked so insidiously against me that the reassurances I relied upon came to be tested. At fifty-six, I had to accept that my left foot could no longer be part of my body. The amputation was successful, but now, walking with my companion was a challenge and required me to rely on the strength of Jesus to support me every step I tried to take with a newly fitted prosthetic. It was not my first or only crisis up to that point, but a harbinger of what was ahead. The following year, I broke my hip and had to deal with the pain that the body can afflict on the mind and the soul when severe dysfunction offends how our organs are designed to work.

Through it all, my strength and spiritual comfort endured without weakening. I never prayed for some miraculous divine intervention but just for successful treatment and, most of all, that the needed strength and courage would never fail me. Most of all, I relied on the simple words of that favorite psalm, "Lord, I place my trust in you."

I feared that something would happen in the future that would render all my experiences up to this point merely a prelude to what was to happen next. And sure enough, that is what happened.

On the evening of December 8, 2008, I tripped over a doorstep, fell backward, shattered my elbow, and broke my hip. The injuries were not life-threatening but entirely debilitating. The physical repair was uncertain. Would I be permanently disabled, far beyond the limitations I had up to that point learned to manage? Would I ever walk again in some fashion? Would I lose forever the use of my right arm? And how would I tolerate the pain I was feeling and would have to endure even if the treatment was successful? Was this finally the end of my valuable life? I never needed my faithful companion more than at that moment, trying to get up after my fall.

Most people—even believers—question their faith at some point. Not just religious people. We all have faith—in some form—that keeps us going, makes us resist giving up entirely, and makes us hope for a future. Some people give up their faith, frustrated by its seeming temporary or without substance. The thing we ask of faith is that it can stand the test. When the "fall," as I call it, intruded into my life, that was the moment when my faith was tested beyond anything that had happened before, for I had no idea that I would ever get up from the fall.

I woke up that night in the hospital after many hours of surgery. I could not move except for a few fingers on the side that had not been injured. I was frightened but most of all angry. There is another psalm I had never prayed before, which is the one that is so spontaneously on everyone's lips in such a moment, "Why me, Lord? Why is this happening to me?" It is easy to feel so abandoned, on one's own, without help, and most of all without that companion who had always seemed so close. So all I could do was call out, "Lord, I trust you." Defiant words to say at such a moment, but habit had taught me to say that at every moment. And so, with anger and fear and on the edge of despair, I asked for strength and courage to get through what I was unwillingly confronting. I had nowhere else to turn.

I traveled a long journey from childhood innocence to this adult crisis. I recovered, thank God, but diminished from my former physical condition. As the years continue to roll by, I can sense how my physical stamina and overall health are slowly passing from my body as old age and diabetes continue to wear me down.

But my relationship with the ever-present Jesus, I feel, is only deepening as I become more familiar with his own human experience and passage through death into a new life that makes it possible for him to be ever at my side.

It is in him that I place my trust and find my strength and courage.

***

I met Tracy about a year ago and was impressed with her knowledge and genuine respect for her clients. The lessons in this story can be applied to any professional career or situation. The author explains what makes a successful dietician; our introduction can emphasize the broader relevance of these invaluable insights for anyone.

Nourishing Confidence: A Journey in Dietetics
Tracy Palmatier, RD, LDN

At the age of twenty-eight, I returned to college to pursue a second degree in nutrition, driven by a deep desire to make a meaningful impact in the lives of others through preventive measures. What became evident to me is that this profession entails far more than I initially anticipated—it is about nurturing my capacity to inspire and empower clients to enact meaningful transformations in their lives. Being an effective dietitian cultivates confidence in ourselves and those we serve.

In dietetics, confidence extends far beyond self-assurance. It encompasses a belief in the efficacy of evidence-based nutrition interventions and a genuine trust in our ability to effect positive change. Furthermore, positive experiences and outcomes enhance our confidence as professionals, reinforcing our belief in our skills and expertise.

I have cultivated my confidence by honing my knowledge and skills to form the foundation of my professional identity. Dietitians undergo extensive education and training to acquire expertise in nutrition science, therapeutic diets, counseling techniques, and behavior-change strategies. We stay abreast of the latest research findings and evidence-based guidelines, ensuring our recommendations are grounded in scientific integrity. This unwavering commitment to excellence instills confidence within us and our clients, who rely on us as trusted sources of information and support.

Confidence transcends knowledge to encompass effective communication and interpersonal skills.

As practitioners, we must establish rapport with clients, foster trust, and create a supportive environment conducive to change. These goals require active listening, empathy, and cultural competence—practices and qualities that empower clients to voice their concerns, preferences, and aspirations. By acknowledging everyone's unique circumstances and lived experiences, we validate their journey toward health and empower them to take ownership of their well-being.

Confidence in dietetics is synonymous with humility—a recognition of the inherent limitations of our knowledge and the dynamic nature of human health. We approach each interaction with a spirit of humility, acknowledging that our role as facilitators of change is not to dictate but to collaborate, educate, and empower. By embracing a growth mindset and continuous learning, we remain steadfast in our commitment to excellence and strive to exceed the expectations of those we serve.

Confidence is a practice and journey of self-discovery, empowerment, and growth.

Registered dietitians have the privilege and responsibility to inspire confidence in ourselves and our clients, fostering wellness, resilience, and vitality. By embodying the principles of confidence, humility, and compassion, we empower individuals to nourish their bodies, minds, and spirits—one bite at a time.

We illuminate the path toward optimal health and well-being through our dedication to excellence and empowering others.

***

Discipline Is Liberation

On New Year's Eve 1989, I sat in an attorney's office, signing papers for my second divorce. I was overwhelmed with disbelief and uncertainty about my next steps.

During those whirlwind twelve years, I experienced many wonderful things. I was blessed with two more beautiful children. I traveled the world, started my commercial insurance agency, invested in a floral business, and made significant strides. Yet it wasn't enough. The relationship became increasingly difficult, profoundly affecting my family and me.

I struggled with confidence, feeling mentally beaten and misunderstood. My insurance business was failing, and I didn't know where to turn. I refinanced my home, leveraging everything from my life insurance to other valuable items. It was a nightmare. I wanted to turn to my father, but I hesitated since he was older and had already done so much for me. My mom had passed away a few years earlier, and I didn't want to worry or burden him further.

I desperately needed an answer, and it came unexpectedly from watching Jane Fonda's workout tapes. Needing to relieve stress, I began exercising with them. The exercise cleared my mind, and getting in shape was a bonus. I distinctly remember Jane Fonda saying, "Discipline is liberation." At that moment, I realized I needed to get my act together. With discipline, I could move on and become the best version of myself. I knew that with focus and dedication, I could regain my confidence and positively shape my life and my family's.

It's been quite a journey. Time passed, but I remained focused. My father died suddenly in January 1994. Later that year, in June, I met the love of my life, Greg. He lived in Massachusetts, and I was in New Jersey, leading to a long-distance relationship for over four years.

Looking back, it was wild, and I still wonder how I managed everything. In the early spring of 1998, Greg asked me to marry him. We've had many trials and tribulations, but our marriage has been wonderful. Greg, who had no children, took on my family with grace and love. We've been married for twenty-six years, and everyone is doing well.

Patience, dedication, and discipline have given me the confidence to move forward and instruct my children the same.

CHAPTER 3

The Journey Continues

For what it's worth ... it's never too late,
or in my case too early, to be
whoever you want to be. There is no time limit.
Start whenever you want.
You can change or stay the same. There are no rules to this thing.
We can make the best or the worst of it.
I hope you make the best of it.
I hope you see things that startle you. I hope you
feel things you've never felt before. I hope you meet
people who have a different point of view.
I hope you live a life you're proud of, and if you're not,
I hope you have the courage to start over again.

—**F. Scott Fitzgerald**, *"For What It's Worth"*

Christine is a remarkable, warm individual. She is a licensed massage and bodywork therapist who makes me feel at peace after a massage. The author's message is that confidence can still be found within oneself, even amid trauma and emptiness. Cultivating and sustaining confidence causes a profound shift in circumstances and perspectives, sometimes in drastic measures. Remember, it's possible to forge new paths rather than erasing the old ones.

Confidence Is a Journey
Christine Chase

Confidence has been a journey to recapture my authentic self.

When people say I am confident, I smile to myself. I wasn't always this way. I grew up the opposite of confident.

The youngest of six in an alcoholic family, I learned all the traits of a child of alcoholic parents—fear, insecurity, lack of trust, and anxiety, to name a few.

My life was one of survival rather than growth.

When I was very young, my mother told me, "Don't open your mouth; no one cares what you have to say." So my silence began. *No one* included my mother. Alone and without a voice, it was an isolated place to be.

My home life was scary, and the world was scary.

I made unconscious agreements with myself to be safe. Stay out of the way, be quiet, and never voice an opinion. All I knew was the dysfunction I had learned to survive. I carried it around like a suitcase and unpacked it into adulthood.

The problem with unconscious agreements made at the time of trauma is that we are not aware of them. Being invisible and silent no longer served me, and life became difficult. The world demands participation, and I didn't function well. Trauma had taken my core. I had no sense of self.

At age twenty-seven, the birth of my son provided a threshold I could cross into confidence. Our original innocence contains truth that is deeper into our sense of self than our trauma. His innocence and wholeness mirrored the parts of myself I had lost. His presence reopened my heart, which had been closed for a long time. I always say that my son saved my life, believing it to be true.

Confidence is the miracle of birth.

I became aware that my husband's behavior had become unacceptable, and my relationship with him was over. I could see that I was repeating the same patterns I had learned as a child to survive my marriage.

I went back to work and back to school. I was determined to be independent, and I eventually filed for divorce. For the first time, I felt a strong sense of self.

"What will you do without all my money?" he said arrogantly.

I remember this moment clearly. I was standing in our dining room, looking out the window into the yard. A vision of freedom and childlike play came to mind. "Cartwheels," was my reply. "I am going to do cartwheels."

Confidence is the courage to leap into the unknown.

With my childhood and marriage behind me and a precious little boy by my side, I began searching for the missing pieces of myself that I couldn't name.

I studied Reiki, Buddhism, yoga, meditation, hypnosis, massage therapy, and shamanism.

Reiki felt natural and nurturing. It allowed me to understand that we are all connected energetically and always will be.

Yoga unveiled more layers of myself, and I began to understand the philosophy and gain self-knowledge.

Kundalini, the yoga of awareness, gave me the courage to examine myself and gain confidence systematically.

Massage therapy offered the nurturing touch I did not receive as a child and deeply connected me to my physical body.

Confidence is gained from knowledge, personal experience, and the ability to apply it to life.

A few years ago, I met a shaman and discovered soul retrieval.

Soul retrieval is a journey back to our original trauma, where we uncover the unconscious agreements we made with ourselves to be safe. We come to understand how these agreements are holding us back. We write new agreements that serve us so we may go forward living full and happy lives.

These new agreements allowed me to change how I felt about myself. My view of the world changed when I changed how I felt about myself. I let go of fear. I could see that happiness is my birthright and that I was born whole. I belong to myself, and I belong in the world.

From this experience, I began to study shamanism. I will be certified in shamanic energy healing so that I can share this wonderful modality, which has greatly and positively impacted my life.

Confidence is knowing that we are the same and we all belong.

For me, confidence has many layers. It is not a personality trait or a projection. It lies deep in my core. My confidence has grown through the many changes in my life, in listening to my inner voice, my innate knowing and trust in myself, and my connection to the universe. It is a sense that I have a purpose, and it cultivates a strong desire to help others.

Love is the biggest catalyst for confidence. Without the people who truly loved and cared for me, I would not have thrived. I believe that when we are loved, we can expand beyond self-perceived limitations. We must discover love within ourselves. Self-love, love for and from others, is the foundation from which confidence is built.

Confidence is love!

***

Dream and Think Big

Growing up, my mom had a quote from Eleanor Roosevelt that she always reminded me of. It read, "Do one thing every day that scares you."

Wouldn't you agree taking a risk is scary?

On October 5, 1995, I decided to take a risk. I started my small business and signed an agreement to be an independent beauty consultant for Mary Kay Cosmetics. Really? Yes, really.

I spent the last twenty-five years in the commercial insurance business, selling insurance to long-haul truckers, restaurants, and manufacturers.

Now I was selling lipstick, lotion, and lifestyle.

I met a Mary Kay cosmetics gal two days before signing this agreement at a chamber networking meeting. We exchanged cards, and then she said, "Jean, we're having a makeover meeting with a guest speaker tomorrow night. I would love for you to come and bring a couple of friends."

She must have seen something on my face that screamed, "I need fun!" Those last two years had been a nightmare. I went through a divorce, my insurance business was failing miserably, and my father, best friend and mentor, died suddenly of a heart attack. I was beat up, chewed up, and fed up.

So I went to that makeover meeting. I brought two friends; we were the hecklers in the back of the room. The consultants up front were so happy. Then they went on stage, winning prizes for selling lipstick.

It was when the guest speaker, Mary Kay national director, a six-foot-one vibrant woman, got up and spoke. She looked directly at me and talked about working at JC Penney selling shoes for $2.90 an hour, when she was approached by a Mary Kay consultant. She then said, "Taking that risk changed my life." She had been in the Mary Kay business for fifteen years and earned ten pink Cadillacs.

Her income in the past year was well into six figures, which made me sit up and listen. She said the business was about more than cosmetics and women helping women succeed. She ended her thoughts by saying you need to *dream and think big.*

This brought back fond memories.

I remember jumping off the bus and running home to watch a program called *Queen for a-Day* with my mom. We had a thirteen-inch black-and-white TV. I would gaze at the women in sequin gowns gliding down the stairs and going across the stage to win a washer and dryer. This isn't what excited me—it was the beautiful women in their sequin gowns.

I would tell my mama, "I want to be one of those gals."

She would tell me, "Sweetie, with desire and vision, you can have anything you want. Dream and think big."

I have carried those words with me my entire life.

Fast-forward to the Mary Kay Conference in July 2001. Standing at the top of the stairs in my sequin gown, waiting for my name to be called, I glided down and crossed the stage to pick up the keys to my first pink Cadillac. I could hear my mother's voice saying, "Jean, dream and think big. Dream and think big."

Anything is possible if you are willing to do the work.

With vision and desire, you need to believe in yourself,

Most of all, like the national director and my mama, said, "Dream and think big."

Let me ask you. What risks do you need to take? What commitment are you willing to make, and what agreements are waiting to be signed?

Courage + Action = Confidence.

***

Do what you feel in your heart to be right—
for you'll be criticized anyway.
    —Eleanor Roosevelt

I've known Jessica, this rock star, since 2012. Her passion and drive are unmistakable. Viewing a no as a failure can instill a fear so intense that one avoids risk altogether. Alternatively, it can be seen as "I've given my all, and now it's time to pivot (for now)." There's plenty to learn from this perspective!

Doubt to Dominance: Mastering the Art of High-End Design Sales

Jessica Harling

When I started in the family window-covering business as a showroom manager, everyone told me I would be a great salesperson. "You're beautiful and an actress; it's just like being on stage," they'd insist. "You're going to kill it in the field," they'd say. At every insistence, I met them with resistance. "What does being beautiful and being an actress have to do with sales? Plus, I work in the showroom; I don't have to do sales!" I'd respond. Then, one day, the inevitable happened: I was promoted from my comfortable showroom position into the terrifying world of outside sales. In my family's mind, I had to get sales under my belt to lead the company into the future because the most respected professionals were legacy employees who worked every position to get to where they were.

Because of their core values of "educate the mind" and my total fear surrounding sales, they gave me all the resources I needed to be successful. They flew me across the country to shadow million-dollar salespeople in the industry; had me attend numerous sales conferences, as well as both on-site and online group training; hired a one-on-one sales coach from the nation's first decorating franchise to work with me weekly; found me leads for the most lucrative parts of downtown Chicago in $3 million+ condos and homes, and more! Most salespeople would kill for the resources and opportunities I was given. I went on four to five weekly appointments for over six months ... without getting one single sale. I wasn't even getting lucky ... and my fears became my reality.

One day, in a personal state of frustration that nothing was working, my sales coach suggested shopping the competition. I scheduled three home appointments with competitors. I went to approximately ten different showrooms in the Chicago area that I perceived as my most significant competitors. The mission was to uncover what they were doing differently over two weeks. On each undercover appointment, I gave the salesperson the same set of challenges for them to overcome and pricing to compare. After every appointment, I left them with my contact information and an open invitation for them to follow up with me after I had received my other estimates.

The first person who came to my home stumbled in with many sample books, looking disheveled, couldn't remember our initial conversation, and was more interested in the dog that belonged to my roommate than in me or my project. The second person forgot to measure a window, then continuously argued that they remembered a space when I asked them to return to the room and look for themselves.

The third insulted me on my style selection, saying it was "too dated" and "no one does this anymore." Then they tried to do a hard close and give me an extra 5 percent if I purchased with them today. Because I shared which competitor was still coming out, they offered an additional 5 percent.

After meeting with the salespeople, I thought, *That is my competition? That is who I have been losing jobs to this whole time?* So, after two weeks of being a detective and shopping around, I went to my next appointment feeling like a peacock. I focused on the client and their lifestyle, and when I was asked the question, "Why should I do business with you?" I smiled and proudly said, "Because I know I'm the *best* in the market and part of the family. We've been in business for over eighty years and have seen businesses come and go, so I guarantee you that even if I ever leave, you will know where to find me because family is forever." With that, they handed me a check to move forward. That check snowballed into an 86 percent closing rate by the end of the year and $350k in sales based on being on the road for two days a week for the rest of the six months.

So what changed in the two weeks of shopping for the competition?

I had the same good looks, the same educational experiences, the same expert proficiency in product information, the same sales process, and the same resources and support. What was the difference? Confidence.

I learned from this experience that you need the confidence to tell your story.

The script I kept repeating in my head was "I can't," "I won't," "I don't," but as soon as I rewrote it to "I can, I will, I do," everything changed. My other takeaway was to minimize the technical information that overwhelms a client or is my job to handle. Jean MacDonald says, "Sell the sizzle, not the steak." I bored my clients with the technical product information, thinking it would show them my expertise. They only cared about how they would feel when the project was over, looking at their beautiful space. Technical knowledge is still essential, as it saves you from making mistakes in the execution of the sale. But confidence sells the job, not your technical knowledge. Confidence closes the deal.

After I applied those takeaways, the most significant attribute that set me apart—when all the other competitors got into peacock mode, vying for our client's attention—was my follow-up skills. While shopping for the competition, I left my contact information with over two dozen businesses. I make it my mission to follow up with every prospect until I get a yes or no. So, although sheer confidence undoubtedly helped me get in the door, that alone didn't enable me to sell 86 percent of my deals. Follow-up closed those deals. The two are a winning—and necessary—combination.

The moral of this story is that sometimes you lack confidence because you hold yourself up to a higher standard than you need to. It can be helpful to find out that your competition (or even your role model) isn't as perfect as you imagine, and then you can give yourself permission to recognize and tell yourself all your good qualities.

***

Nurturing Confidence and Bonds through Business

You never know when a challenge might transform into an opportunity. I want to share a personal story that became a valuable life lesson for my daughter and me.

In the fall of 1995, my daughter Laura came home from school excited about her eighth-grade math class assignment.

"Mom!" she exclaimed. "Our math project for the semester is to run a business. What should I do?"

I owned an insurance agency, which didn't seem like an ideal choice for her project. We needed something more engaging. After discussing it that evening, I suggested we sleep on it and talk again the next day.

Business is fundamentally about people connecting with other people.

I wasn't sure what to suggest, but I hoped for inspiration at a networking meeting the following day. After chatting with several attendees, a woman approached me. "Where did you get your awesome shoes?" she asked.

Her compliment caught me off guard, and we began talking. I mentioned my commercial insurance agency, and she introduced herself as Kate, a sales director for Mary Kay Cosmetics.

Although I knew little about the company, having only received some samples months earlier, Kate invited me to a special event to learn more and meet other inspiring women.

This was the perfect solution for Laura's project and me. Laura was thrilled. In October, I started a direct-selling business alongside my insurance business.

It was an incredible journey for both Laura and me. She was diligent and helpful, working in my office, handling paperwork, cleaning cosmetic mirrors, and preparing my event bags. She also assisted with making holiday gift baskets and helped during open-house events.

I paid Laura six dollars an hour, half of which went to her and the other half into her college savings. Laura always encouraged me to get out and sell as her bank account grew. I was proud to see her manage the paperwork and organize the office.

Laura's school project turned out to be a tremendous success. We hosted makeup sessions before dances, where she did everyone's makeup and taught them about good skincare. She brought products to school for her classmates to try and organized mother/daughter events.

It was an excellent lesson in entrepreneurship, giving Laura a sense of worth and involvement in the bigger picture as our business flourished.

The rewards were often priceless.

The most rewarding moment of our partnership came at the end of her senior year when I handed her a $3,500 check—the money we had saved over the years from her work. This provided ample spending money for college and was a tangible testament to her hard work and dedication.

Beyond the financial rewards, the life lessons she acquired were invaluable. The company I represented taught me to "fail forward," a lesson I passed on to her. Laura, an extraordinary athlete, learned to set goals, commit, persevere, and strive for excellence through this project. She became a top pole vaulter, ranking number two in Western Massachusetts and the top ten in New England in high school.

Laura attended the University of North Carolina at Chapel Hill and has built an outstanding career in medical devices. She also maintained her entrepreneurial spirit, running various rewarding side businesses. She is now married with two beautiful children.

Why is this story significant? It highlights the power of confidence! Reflecting on positive experiences can profoundly affect our outcomes. Sharing our confidence with future generations and building it together is crucial.

If you own a small business, why not involve your children? Life skills are invaluable; working together fosters a strong bond and a sense of responsibility. Your child can take pride in contributing to your business and its successes.

Who could you influence and build their confidence?

***

Six years ago, I met Jennifer through networking, and our connection was immediate. She's become not just a dear friend but also a valued mentor. The author's message serves as a poignant reminder that we possess the power to alter our paths, seeking out what brings us joy and, in doing so, nurturing our confidence as we journey forward.

From Learning to Earning
Jennifer Halloran, PhD

Unlike most people who spend their twenties and thirties finding and establishing a career, starting their retirement funds, and saving for a house, I spent eleven years in graduate school.

I had always wanted a career as a professor, teaching English literature to undergraduates, preferably at a small liberal arts college. When I started graduate school, the people around me kept saying it was a distinguished career path because all the tenured professors would be retiring just as I finished, opening many jobs for new PhDs.

However, two things changed my planned trajectory when I graduated and started working as a postdoc at Duke University. First, the tenured professors did not retire after all. Many stayed well past their retirement dates, and those who did retire were often replaced with part-time, untenured instructors who barely made enough to live on.

The other thing that happened was realizing that academia wasn't a healthy place for me. I loved the students and our interactions, but the office politics and increasingly dire job market made the struggle to secure a job so stressful that I was making myself sick.

So, here I was, with a PhD in English literature, becoming what people called a "washout" from the only career I'd ever dreamed of. I had no idea of anything I was good at besides teaching and researching, and the thought of doing either made me physically ill.

The words of poet Mary Oliver constantly rang in my ears, "Tell me, what is it you plan to do with your one wild and precious life?"

I knew I wanted to be in a profession that made a noticeable difference in others' lives. Teaching was fun, but students came and went; it was hard to know whether anything I taught had changed someone. For this second career, I wanted to see that I was improving things for people.

The answer came from inside my own family.

My mother, a registered nurse for over forty years, had retired. But, like many great nurses, she wasn't interested in slowing down. Instead, her brain had been working overtime, thinking about how nurses' knowledge and experience needed to be shared. Her thoughts led her to start a business, Everybody Needs A Nurse, a patient advocate.

Rather than take up knitting in a rocking chair, my mother started networking with other businesspeople, discovering the legalities and nuances of setting up a business. She met with SCORE advisors and joined the local chamber of commerce. Even when I was still working at Duke, I'd go with her to networking events and health fairs, starting to craft a message to people about the benefits of working with a patient advocate.

For many months, though, we had no clients. Although I understood how much a registered nurse as a health care advocate would improve things for someone dealing with complex medical issues, we had to do a lot of educating to get people familiar with what a patient advocate is and how they can help.

I wanted so much to work at the business with my mom. We have a great relationship, and after the cut-throat world of academics, I wanted to work with someone who supported me. But the money wasn't coming in, and I needed to earn.

Then, within two weeks, Everybody Needs A Nurse got six clients. Suddenly, we were doing well, and my mom needed my organizational support. I was so excited to come aboard, but then I hit my next hurdle—I didn't know much about the world of health care, particularly senior care, which is the specialty of Everybody Needs A Nurse.

This crossroads was where I used the skills and practices I had developed in my PhD.

I created my curriculum on senior care. I read articles and books. I met with many people who worked in this arena and gleaned best practices from them. I created message after message about what we do. Our current message is "Everybody Needs A Nurse to support seniors and their families through the health challenges of aging." We make weekly home visits, accompany clients to doctor visits, manage medications, and communicate regularly with family, becoming their eyes and ears on the situation.

I learned that I love this branch of health care.

Our work makes a massive difference in the lives of seniors and their families. I feel a bond between my family caring for clients and the families of the clients we look after. I also learned that I love the world of small business. Through my business, I have made many great connections and friends. As an introverted academic, I would never have imagined being outgoing was part of my path!

I'm also working on leadership and helping other women transition to owning and running a small business.

I'm never bored—there's always something more to learn and to do. Another message to craft, another family to help, another way to connect. I feel proud of what I've done with my "wild and precious life." Leaping out of my first career is what made it all happen.

The confidence it gave me has given me the journey of my life.

CHAPTER 4

Developing Confidence

Conquering Adversity: A Journey
of Support and Confidence

The following are steps for developing confidence after failure:

- Evaluate mistakes to understand areas of improvement.
- Develop a positive mindset to turn challenges into opportunities.
- Research and explore innovative methods and approaches.
- Be proactive in seeking guidance and advice.

Life can throw many curveballs. It wouldn't be life without ups and downs. It has been brought to my attention many times that families are struggling with mental health and substance abuse with either a partner, family member, or child.

When our loved ones are going through tough times, sometimes we need to put our feelings on hold and give all our strength to them. We must instill belief in them until they can believe in themselves.

Here are some strategies that can build confidence and help someone move forward:

- *Use consistent positive reinforcement.* Regularly remind them of their strengths and past achievements, helping them see their potential.
- *Actively listen.* Ensure they are heard and their feelings are valid, fostering a safe space for open communication.
- *Set small, achievable goals.* Set small, manageable goals to help them rebuild their self-esteem and regain a sense of accomplishment.
- *Model confidence.* Demonstrate confidence in your actions and decisions by providing a living example for them to emulate.
- *Encourage healthy relationships.* Focus on surrounding them with supportive friends and family members who contribute positively to their lives.
- *Seek professional help.* Seek professional counseling when needed, showing them it's okay to ask for help.
- *Celebrate progress.* No matter how small, celebrate every bit of progress, reinforcing their belief in their ability to change and grow.

If a loved one is struggling, believe in them and tell them constantly how much you love them. Find the talent or skill in them that can change the picture and bring them the joy they need.

As I said before, confidence has many faces, and sometimes, when we forget what we need and help others find success, we reap the rewards we are looking for in ourselves.

***

Building Confidence One Cold Call at a Time

Bet on yourself.
Work on yourself and love others.
Have the courage to take the next steps.
Change your mind to change your life.

As you read this book, you may recall stories that illustrate what builds your confidence or tears it down. Today, while I was having coffee with a friend, she reminded me of a story I shared at a speaking event, which I realized would be perfect for this book.

In my early years selling commercial insurance, I vividly remember my boss asking me to cold-call businesses. This terrified me. I had no confidence in knocking on doors, asking when their insurance policies were up for renewal, getting contact names, and informing them I would follow up.

It didn't matter how I felt about it though. Off we went. The insurance agency was in Morristown, New Jersey, with many stores nearby. My boss would stop at a retail business, and we would walk in together. He would demonstrate how it should be done. Some owners were gracious and willing to help, while others were uninterested.

After visiting several places, we got in the car and drove to another area of town, repeating the process. Then my boss said, "It's your turn. I'll wait in the car while you gather the information." We pulled up in front of a locally owned pharmacy. It had a large plate-glass window, allowing a clear view of the pharmacist working in the back.

I walked in, holding my breath, feeling anxious and scared. The woman at the front counter was lovely, and I asked if her boss was in and if I could speak with him. She directed me to the pharmacist at the back of the store.

I approached the pharmacist, still apprehensive but ready to ask the questions my boss had asked. The pharmacist, busy filling orders, finally asked, "What can I do for you?" I took a deep breath and gave him my pitch. He replied, "Many people from insurance companies stop by wanting my business. What makes you different?"

With a tentative smile, I said, "Do you see the guy sitting in the car outside? That's my boss. He asked me to come in and chat with the owner to gather the information for your insurance. I may get fired if I don't return with this information."

He laughed and said, "Really? Since you were brave enough to do this, I'll give you the information you need, but I doubt I'll ever see you again."

I thanked him and told him I would return in the fall before his policies were up for renewal to gather more information for a quote. He mentioned he was unhappy with his current insurance agent and that if I returned and did a good job, I could earn his business.

Feeling great, I returned to the car and handed the information to my boss. He was floored! I used the same approach at the next several places we visited, and the leads started pouring in. My boss was elated and wondered how a newbie did so well. But I didn't let him in on my secret!

I returned to the pharmacy in the fall. The owner chuckled when he saw me because he anticipated I would return. He became one of my best clients and later opened several more pharmacies. Because of my tenacity and confidence, I learned that stepping out of your comfort zone can lead to remarkable success. It was a practice that built relationships and helped build a business.

What steps do you need to take that make you sweat or glow?

The confidence we gain when we step out of our comfort zone can be invaluable for life's journey.

***

A Life-Changing Experience

We need to find and use whatever resources are available to help us build and maintain our confidence. For me, Toastmasters was crucial in helping me grow into the person I wanted to become.

My journey began with Toastmasters almost twenty-four years ago. I had no idea how this would change my life and open the door to many extraordinary opportunities. For those who have never heard of Toastmasters, it is an organization that started in 1924 to aid people in developing their communication and leadership skills.

A classified ad in our local hometown paper read, "Come to our club and learn the art of speaking, develop your leadership skills, and make some great friends." This looked interesting, and I went to my first Toastmasters meeting on a cold February evening. The meeting was held at a senior care center. Several members greeted me when I arrived. A large dining room was being set up, and I jumped right in, moving tables around and helping them get ready for the evening.

A crowd of about fifteen was getting ready for the meeting. Suddenly, the door in the back of the room opened, and several senior residents who lived at the care center came and found a seat. I had no idea what to expect, but I felt welcome and ready to learn.

The meeting was organized. That evening, there were three speakers. One of them, Joe, a longtime resident, got up with his walker and proceeded to the lectern. Joe shared a touching story about his life, including losing his wife after sixty years of marriage. His story was so compelling there wasn't a dry eye in the audience.

I realized then that this was a wonderful place to learn and grow my confidence. I saw many opportunities that evening and felt very welcome.

There were two other guests along with me. We were asked for our opinion of the meeting and to come back and get involved. I left feeling so good and thought it was just what I needed to build my self-esteem and confidence.

This new adventure I started twenty-four years ago has given me so much. Whether sharing stories, running a meeting, or perfecting my leadership skills, this is the place to be. This may sound like a commercial, but I will tell you I have given this gift to many over the years and have seen them ignited and more confident. You'll find a supportive, learn-by-doing environment that allows you to learn at your own pace.

If this scares you, I understand. Eleanor Roosevelt said, "Do one thing that scares you every day." I know speaking ranks up there with the fear of flying or death.

Another way to build confidence is to take a class, get involved in an organization, or volunteer in the community. Getting involved, participating, and bringing others with you will raise your self-esteem and confidence.

Courage + Action = Confidence.

***

The folks we meet along life's path often equip us with what is ahead. Sharon is one such person—a beacon of positivity who uplifts everyone around her. Here are some valuable lessons the author imparts, trusting that inner voice that asks, "Why not?" Embrace ongoing learning, be it in your career or hobbies. Concentrate on what truly matters for your growth and development.

Listening to Your Inner Voice
Sharon Hill, MBA

How could I have been so stupid? Why didn't I go to class instead of playing cards daily at the student union? When my counselor advised me that my 1.7 GPA meant I was kicked out of college, I felt like a total failure.

My mother expected me to graduate as a successful schoolteacher, secretary, or nurse. My future looked bleak. As a Black girl with no college education, I felt powerless to control my destiny. Confidence? Forget about it. I was nothing.

So how did a young lady carrying that much personal baggage eventually become president of four nonprofit organizations, start three entrepreneurial businesses, serve on the Toastmasters International Board of Directors, host a radio show for six years, write five books, and chair a county board of economic development?

Call it fate, destiny, or luck that developed my confidence. As a lowly secretary with no hope of advancing to a position of power, I took a chance that began my life change. One day, the gentleman who serviced the office equipment suggested I interview for a marketing position at Fortune 500 IBM. He must have seen something in me that I did not know I possessed. I had no college degree but was going to night school. Me? IBM? No way.

But a voice within me said, "Why not? What have I got to lose?" Because of the voice within me, I updated my wardrobe to look businesslike and went for the interview. Imagine my shock when, after two interviews, I got a phone call offering me the job on the condition that I continue going to college and graduate.

Above all, I learned to love myself.

Although I was thrilled beyond belief to be working for IBM, my confidence was rock bottom. My coworkers already had college degrees, wore designer clothes, sported expensive jewelry, and drove fancy cars. Deep down, I still considered myself unworthy because I had none of those finer things in life.

Perhaps because of my insecurity about my abilities, I applied myself to learn everything I could about my job responsibilities. Between going to school and working, I had no time for foolishness. As the years passed, I became the go-to woman for advice and training. I finally earned my bachelor's degree and was honored to be on the dean's list, then earned an MBA. These successes began my confidence building. I saw that those coworkers around me who I was admiring did not focus on learning as much as I did. Customers asked for me because I could relate to them better than many of my peers.

What followed were promotions every eighteen months. With each new job position, my insecurities faded. My confidence grew. I realized that I had talents, was a leader, and would let no one put me down. I spoke up, demanded respect, and was a servant leader. Each year, I was in the top 10 percent of IBM managers. In addition to my worldwide marketing management responsibilities, I was elected chair of the IBM Black Diversity Network Group at IBM's most prominent site. Gone was the young lady who carried so much baggage and felt like a failure.

After IBM, I decided to work on my bucket list. My reputation preceded me. I was asked to lead boards of directors and host a radio show, and I accepted. I sold my books at speaking engagements. I joined Toastmasters to become a more vital speaker and was ultimately elected to the Toastmasters Board of Directors.

What gave me confidence?

- staying focused on what was expected from me and applying myself
- watching, listening, and learning
- brushing off negative self-talk and taking bold steps without fear

Above all, I learned to love myself.

***

Recipe to Build Confidence

2 cups of courage

3 1/2 cups of belief

2 cups of practicing self-care

3 cups of action

1/2 cup of don't take it personally

1 cup of inspiration

1 cup of practicing self-compassion

2/3 cup of embracing failure

2 cups of no comparing

1 teaspoon of sass (not too much; we do not want to come across as rude)

Throw in some realistic goals.

Mix all the ingredients, then whip for five minutes at high speed until your head spins.

Tap off the beaters and naysayers.

Scrape the bowl to get all the belief you can.

Now add five happy faces who love and support you. Call them, feel the love, and have some give you the "Get your ass moving and keep moving" talk.

Put everything into perspective and breathe. Maybe even get half-baked with a good bottle of wine.

When all is said and done, how do you feel?

Share with others; they may need it more than you.

Remember, Courage + Action = Confidence.

Use it, share it, and repeat.

Optional—adjust ingredients at your discretion.

CHAPTER 5

Finding the Fire

What sets your soul on fire?
—**Ashley McBride**

Judy is someone I've known for seven years. She has always been forward-thinking and full of creativity. She constantly connects with people and considers others' needs. I contacted her to write this piece to help us discover clarity, peace, and inspiration through journaling and vision boards.

A Journey of Self-Discovery: Vision Boards and Journaling
Judy Harrelson

I've always found inspiration to be a far more inviting companion than motivation. Motivation feels like a chore, something tethered to consequences and obligations. But inspiration? It's a different world filled with joy, readiness, and eagerness to embrace a project.

Imagine, if you will, a spiral. Nature offers countless examples: seashells, plant tendrils, and ferns unfurling. We have a choice in how we follow this spiral. We can venture inward, where it can feel constricting and harmful, trapping us in victimhood, unworthiness, and a feeling of being stuck. Or we can follow it outward, where it expands into openness, possibility, and positivity. Starting with an optimistic attitude, gratitude builds confidence and helps me find more things to be grateful for.

I've walked both paths. I know the weight of the downward spiral and the buoyancy of the upward one. It all comes down to the energy we emit—the thoughts we nurture. As the saying goes, "Once you see it, you can't unsee it." So, I ask you, which path will you choose?

In a world filled with anxiety and fear, much of which we cannot control, I've come to realize the importance of focusing on what we can control. It's a process that begins with the imagination.

Only a fraction of people—about 5 percent—write down what they want in life. Astonishingly, over 95 percent of those who do see their dreams materialize. It's a powerful testament to the influence of visualization.

If you seek change, refrain from describing your current reality unless you are content with it.

Complaining about our circumstances tends to anchor us in more of the same. It's not the situations that make us unhappy; it's the stories we tell ourselves about them. Awareness, then, becomes our greatest ally. The link between science and spirituality is that everything in the universe is energy. It's the reality of life, and we can tap into it.

So, how do we harness this power of the mind constructively? Enter the vision board— a tangible visual where our desires, energy, and joy come together.

Creating Your Vision Board

1. Gratitude reflection
Begin with gratitude. Consider what you're thankful for in your life right now. Gather images or words that represent these blessings. Visualize how you want your life to start with *being*. One common but harmful misconception in our society is that we must *do* something first; *go, go, do*, then you'll *have* what you want and then be happy. The reality is the other way around. *Be* present, centered, peaceful, and open to possibilities. Then the right things will come into your path for you to *do*. Then you can *have* what you want.

2. Desires and dreams
Next, think about what you'd like to invite into your life. Who do you want to be and why? The when, how, and where is the magic that happens when you declare what you want. Let go and trust. Please focus on the

essence of what you want rather than the specifics of how you think you will get it.

3. Define yourself
Write down words that resonate with who you are or aspire to be. Are you passionate, loving, kind, appreciative?

4. The "why" behind your dreams
Reflect on your purpose. Why do you want these things in your life? What drives your aspirations? Dream *big*.

5. Creative expression
Gather materials that speak to you—magazines, personal photos, drawings, symbols.
Let your creativity flow. Tear out images, words, or phrases from magazines or the web. Trust your instincts.

6. Visualization meditation
When ready to create your board, find a quiet space. Meditate on how you want your life to unfold. Feel the emotions associated with your dreams.

7. Energize your board
Assemble your board, add color, draw, highlight—whatever feels right. Stand back and look at it; how does it make you feel? When you like the way it looks, glue everything to the board.

8. Daily affirmation

Place your vision board where you will see it every day. Be aware when the things on the board manifest in your life.

Embracing the Journey: Journaling Insights

In January 2020, life took an unexpected turn for me. An accident left me with a concussion, stripping away the familiar life of screens and technology. Suddenly, I found myself confined to the simplicity of nature, listening to the birds, seeing the trees (really seeing them), and strolling. My days were simple—eat, walk, rest, repeat.

Talk about being present—it's all I could do! I had to let go of all the planning, thinking, and doing. I had to *be* in the moment.

The Healing Power of Journaling

After a few weeks, I discovered I could write on paper—no electronics needed. This gave me a two-month head start on everyone else in self-isolation with COVID-19. People have spent small fortunes and time away at retreats to "find themselves."

As I reacquainted with pen and paper, I found a sanctuary within journaling. It became a vessel for my thoughts, reflections, and the blossoming of ideas. I realized journaling was not merely about recording events; it was a pathway to understanding, a map to navigate the labyrinth of my mind.

The Art of Letting Go

When it comes to journaling, there's no one-size-fits-all approach. For some, regimented daily entries may be the key. But I write when inspiration strikes or I'm struggling with a question seeking answers.

I write without judgment and let the words flow on the page. Writing becomes a journey, often leading me to destinations I hadn't imagined. It's a release, and usually, I don't know where it's taking me. Be patient with yourself.

Lessons from Reflection

Months later, as I transcribed my journal entries, I found wisdom amid chaos. Here are a few lessons that emerged:

- *Gratitude in presence.* Embracing the moment with gratitude leads to actual presence.
- *Inner resilience.* Discovering a reservoir of resilience within myself.
- *Self-worth.* Recognizing worthiness from within, independent of external validation.
- *Connection and love.* Understanding the difference between seeking approval and genuine connection. We are all connected through God.
- *Balancing heart and mind.* Allowing my heart to lead, finding harmony between intuition and logic.
- *The gift of being.* Presence and attention as gifts to others and ourselves.
- *Listening to intuition.* Trusting in the guidance of God and intuition.

- *Lessons from loved ones.* Cherishing the teachings and memories passed down from my father. Dad was and still is my teacher.
- *Emotional release.* Acknowledging the power of tears. This emotional release helps the physical body heal.
- *Self-compassion.* Learning to love and show compassion to myself first, then extending it to others.
- *Life as a learning journey.* Understanding that life's challenges are opportunities for growth and learning.
- *Connection with nature.* Listening to the dawn chorus of the Carolina wren, roosters, hawks, and crows, watching the sunrise and sunset, and finding solace and connection in the beauty of nature.

Closing Thoughts

In the dance of life, we are both the choreographers and the dancers. Through vision boards and journaling, I've learned to craft my steps intentionally and gracefully. Each word written, each image placed, is a brushstroke in the masterpiece of my life. I invite you to join me on this journey of self-discovery.

Through the vibrant canvas of a vision board or the intimate pages of a journal, you may find the clarity, peace, and inspiration to live your most authentic life.

Inspiration gets your started.
Consistency keeps you going.

***

The Power of Mentorship

In 1997, both my personal and professional journeys were on the rise. After selling my insurance business, I was gearing up for the next chapter with Mary Kay Cosmetics. Despite recognizing the potential of this venture, I grappled with the complexities of managing sales, recruitment, and business development. While confident in my sales skills, I doubted my leadership abilities. Seeking guidance, I was recommended to find a mentor and potentially a coach.

Upon conducting research, I discovered the immense value a coach could offer in bolstering confidence in various aspects of life, whether it be career advancement, personal growth, or skill refinement. I realized that I didn't have to tackle everything alone.

My sales soared, and I propelled myself to remarkable success in leadership. With twelve prestigious signature car awards to my name, including five iconic pink Cadillacs, I excelled as a top producer. I thrived as a mentor and trainer, nurturing high-performing teams nationwide.

Reflecting on my previous career in insurance, I excelled in sales but struggled with leadership. I managed a team of eight people, and the pressure to drive sales while covering expenses felt overwhelming. Unfortunately, I failed to foster the growth and development of my employees' leadership skills. Looking back, I recognize the importance of having a coach or mentor who could provide guidance and support. My insurance agency suffered because I didn't seek help or share my challenges. Pride and stubbornness prevented me from contacting for assistance, leading to significant losses.

When you think of the word mentor, what comes to mind? A wise and trusted counselor? An influential and experienced sponsor? Someone who offers support in achieving your goals? A mentor can embody all these qualities and more. I've had several mentors throughout my lifetime, though initially, I didn't fully grasp the extent of their value.

Over the years, I've understood that these individuals were more than just friends I could lean on during tough times. They listened to my challenges and then, in a supportive and encouraging manner, challenged me to be accountable for overcoming them. Their advice was rooted in wisdom from facing their challenges, and they were proactive problem solvers who pursued their dreams.

Mentors can be found in all walks of life; some may be up-and-coming go-getters, while others offer a seasoned perspective acquired through years of experience.

My mentors have ranged in age from twenty-two to eighty-five, and their expertise spans diverse fields.

For example, my techie mentor, currently the youngest among them, specializes in navigating the wired (and wireless) world that once seemed foreign to me. He helps me resolve technical issues and expand my knowledge of innovative technologies. At the same time, I mentored him in creating business strategies based on my experience, which was a win-win situation for both of us.

Another mentor, whom I initially considered merely a good friend, has provided frank advice and practical business guidance over the years. She knows how to ask the right questions and helps me solve challenges. We have regular monthly discussions where she holds me accountable for following through on our agreed-upon action plans.

Is it time to find a mentor, business strategist, or coach?

Are you prepared to propel yourself, your business, or your career toward greater success? Are you willing to listen to constructive feedback and commit to the action plans a mentor may help you develop?

These are essential questions because a mentor's time is valuable and should not be taken lightly. Know your goals in seeking a mentor or coach, and clearly express what you hope to learn. Be prepared with your questions and take notes during conversations to maximize your mentor's time and expertise.

After spending several years in the Mary Kay business, I realized it was time for a career change. Relocating multiple times had left me yearning for something new. Seeking guidance, I hired a coach who helped me envision a fresh direction. Thanks to her assistance, I've thrived in communication and business strategy for over fifteen years.

I've been fortunate to have many coaches and mentors throughout my journey. Their support has been invaluable, especially at this stage of my career. It's essential not to feel pressured to go alone; people are often willing to help when asked. Over time, I've learned the importance of seeking help without fear.

As you delve into the inspiring stories within this book, you'll meet women I deeply trust and admire. Remember, genuine and effective mentoring relationships are built on trust, open communication, and mutual respect.

To maximize your confidence and personal growth, take the initiative to seek guidance, ask questions, and actively take part in the mentorship or coaching process.

***

Navigating Life's Journey through Shared Wisdom

Every day, our inboxes fill with emails, many hardly worth a glance, yet occasionally, they contain sentiments that resonate deeply within us. One morning, as I greeted the day, I opened an email from my son, Derek. Nestled within was an article about leaving a legacy, a topic close to my heart.

At the top of his message, I found myself moved to tears. "Mom, you are the best; I try to emulate you daily. Have a great one. Love, Derek, a.k.a. Boo Boo," it read.

In response, I conveyed, *"You* are simply the best, head and shoulders above the rest. The secret to success is going from mistake to mistake without losing enthusiasm. Have a fantastic day too. I love you so much, Mom."

Derek came into my life when I was just twenty-two. By twenty-four, I was navigating the waters of divorce. Though times were tough, we faced them together, evolving into a formidable team. Derek became my rock, fiercely protective and unwaveringly supportive. Our bond has always been profound. Even now, our conversations serve as mutual guidance and comfort, though he often lends me his ear more than I offer mine.

Who is that person in your life you can lean on, listen to, and learn from? Reflect on the wisdom and cherished memories they've imparted.

Consider this: who are you sharing your experiences and insights with? Be a mentor, passing on the lesson's life has taught you, for *you* are simply the best, head and shoulders above the rest.

***

Confidence means feeling sure of yourself, your values,
and your abilities. Stay on track to be the best you can be
without dissuasion. Expect to be amazed at the respect
and admiration others will have for you.
—Sharon Hill

***

Gigi is inspiring, and I have known her for about fifteen years. She embodies determination, creativity, and a pioneering spirit. I love how she demonstrates the power of forging ahead despite challenges and using one's unique qualities to shine. The author's suggestions are spot-on. Being creative in overcoming obstacles is a valuable skill. It's about seeing possibilities where others might see limitations and finding innovative solutions to move forward. Thank you, Gigi, for this inspiring story.

Triumphs of a Limb-Difference Trailblazer
Gigi Verrey

As a female professional with a limb difference navigating the world of financial services, my journey has been one of relentless determination and steadfast confidence. I've faced my share of challenges, from the skeptical glances of colleagues to the subtle barriers built into a workplace designed for able-bodied men. Yet every financial plan I conquer and every complex financial issue I decode speaks volumes about my refusal to let physical differences and gender dictate the limits of my professional prowess.

When I first entered the world of finance in 1992, I knew I was stepping into a realm that might not be ready for someone like me. The industry is known for its male-dominated personnel, golf trips, and long lunches—where success was often measured by who you glad-handed instead of ability. But I brought something unique to the table: a perspective sharpened by years of overcoming the unexpected and a resilience forged from the need to innovate constantly. My confidence has grown with each year, not just in my skills but in the knowledge that I am helping to redefine what it means both to be able and to be a woman in a corporate setting in financial services.

This same spirit spills over into my social media presence. I've taken to Instagram @verysmartideas, not just to share my life with one hand but to challenge the preconceptions about disability and help parents with children with limited differences to help them conquer everyday tasks. Social media, with its visual emphasis and instant judgments, is an unlikely place for someone like me to flourish. But I've turned my limb difference into a powerful narrative, a statement that diversity includes many abilities. I craft engaging and authentic content, encouraging conversations beyond likes and shares. It's about representation, about giving a face and a voice to a community often sidelined.

Perseverance is my watchword.

I post with purpose, whether it's an Instagram story that offers a glimpse into my world. With its ever-changing algorithms and fleeting trends, the digital landscape can be fickle, but my commitment to advocacy doesn't waver. I've built a following not with my expertise in finance but by providing a beacon for others with limb differences, showing that our capabilities can stretch as far as our ambitions in our homes and gardens—even when shaking a fun cocktail.

Each day is an exercise in problem-solving and adaptation. In finance, I've had to find new ways to navigate software designed without someone like me in mind. I've become a de facto expert in adaptability, turning every limitation into a chance to innovate. I've sat in meetings where I've had to assert my competence and my ideas, my voice firm, dispelling any doubts about my qualifications. And in these moments, my confidence becomes my shield and my statement!

In social media, the obstacles are less tangible but no less real. I've faced the invisibility that comes with difference and the challenge of cutting through the noise. But I've learned that my story, everyday triumphs, and struggles resonate deeply with people across the globe. My limb difference, once seen as a hurdle, has become a unique selling point, distinguishing my brand and my message.

Through my journey, I've realized that overcoming obstacles isn't about personal success; it's about leading by example. In the high-stakes environment of financial services, I am more than my job title—I am a trailblazer for inclusivity and a testament to the power of perseverance. Every post I share on social media contributes to a larger conversation about diversity, acceptance, love, and the strength of embracing one's uniqueness.

My path has not been easy, but by viewing my challenges as an opportunity to learn and grow, I have marked it with victories that extend beyond my achievements.

I lay the groundwork for a more inclusive future in finance and online with every barrier I dismantle. I stand as proof that with confidence and perseverance, a limb difference is not a deficit but a differentiator, and it is with this conviction that I continue to pave the way forward.

***

I have known Sophia for around one year. She exudes ambition and diligence, earning respect among her peers; her commitment to excellence sets her apart. Her narrative is compelling, revealing her path toward genuine confidence.

Unmasking Confidence: Embracing Authenticity and Strength

Sophia Munson

Many people focus on trying to be unique individuals. But the truth is you don't have to be unique to become exceptional. In my youth, I had a profound aversion to public speaking. I avoided every opportunity to speak up, preferring to fade into the background. I even wrote stories about my desire to vanish into walls.

Unfortunately, my father's career as a foreign service officer meant constant moves and the need to adapt to new environments and friendships. To cope, I learned to fake confidence for survival. I mastered the art of wearing the right smile and responding appropriately, yet I lacked genuine self-assurance beneath it.

My journey toward authentic confidence began unexpectedly with Agatha Christie's works, particularly Miss Marple's adventures. Despite being a charming elderly lady, Miss Marple possessed an uncanny ability to unmask murderers by drawing parallels with characters from her quaint village. Reading these novels as a young adult, I was struck by the notion that people are inherently predictable.

Oddly enough, this realization helped me confront my insecurities. Popular or unpopular, everyone harbored similar fears and doubts, albeit disguised differently. I could dwell on my shortcomings or acknowledge them as universal human traits. It was like "seeing the audience in their underwear" but in a psychological sense.

Adopting the mantra "everyone is the same" (which drives my husband and law partner crazy) allowed me to accept that everyone possesses strengths and weaknesses. This realization reframed my perspective, emphasizing the importance of finding the right support system to complement our attributes.

Even with this mantra in mind, my path to confidence has been challenged. During my early days as an attorney, I found joy connecting with clients and delivering impactful presentations. Yet routine desk work did not spark my enthusiasm. Even though I was shining in my strengths, my employers focused more on my areas for improvement. Slowly, I started holding back on offering suggestions and eventually stopped generating ideas altogether.

Fortunately, my husband intervened. He encouraged me to challenge myself from the confines of my job and join him in establishing our firm. Although this was a daunting move, we shared a vision of fostering an environment where strengths were celebrated over weaknesses.

Taking that leap of faith was terrifying, but we were determined to cultivate a team that thrived on leveraging individual strengths. At our firm, we encourage each member to identify their areas of expertise, whether it is public outreach, organization, drafting, or marketing.

Our ethos revolves around nurturing confidence because while people may be predictable, we can harness our collective potential to create something extraordinary together.

Instead of striving to be unique, focusing on authenticity and leveraging one's strengths can lead to exceptional outcomes. Surrounding oneself with a supportive environment that values individual talents fosters confidence and collective success. Personal growth often requires stepping out of one's comfort zone and taking bold risks.

***

When I met Aishling, I had no idea what being a caregiver meant. The education she has given so many is invaluable in helping our aging population. She has taken her home care business to the next level by helping certified nursing assistants with the proper competency-based education and skills. Her message is clear, "Don't doubt yourself or your abilities."

Believe in Yourself: Lessons from a Home Care Entrepreneur
Aishling Dalton Kelly

Growing up in a family of caregivers, I learned the importance of respect and dignity in caring for seniors. After my parents' passing, I started a home care business. Despite being advised against it, I leaped, eager to make a difference.

I partnered with someone I knew from my daughter's school, thinking his financial background would be beneficial. However, red flags emerged early on. He ignored policies, mishandled funds, and deceived me about business matters. Trusting my gut, I decided to dissolve the partnership and start anew.

I learned valuable lessons when I set up my own company: trust yourself and don't ignore warning signs. I hit my million-dollar target within three years, realizing I never needed a partner; I just needed to believe in myself.

Reflecting on this journey, I now share advice for aspiring entrepreneurs: always trust your instincts, have clear policies, and do due diligence with potential partners. Surround yourself with trustworthy professionals, and never lose sight of your goals.

Today, I lead various associations and initiatives in the health care field, proof that determination and self-belief can lead to success. Years later, my former partner closed the business, but I continue to thrive.

Your thoughts and dreams will become a reality if you believe in yourself and never let anyone talk you out of what you know to be true in your heart.

"Integrity is doing the right thing even when no one is watching" (C. S. Louis).

Don't doubt yourself and your abilities. If you give yourself a chance to grow, you'll be amazed at what you can achieve. Make sure the people you surround yourself with have the same values and the same goals you do.

CHAPTER 6

Building Our Children's Confidence

Children become self-confident when they grow up with
much love and your undivided attention.

Cultivating Confidence: A Grandparent's
Journey through Board Games

In today's fast-paced world, it is easy to get swept up in distractions, losing sight of the simple joys found in genuine connection. How often do we truly immerse ourselves in the present moment, free from the pull of screens and notifications?

On Sundays after church, I sometimes invite my granddaughter, who is four, to come over and spend time with me and Pop Pop. We do crafts, bake, watch a movie with a snack, go outside for a walk with the dog, or go to the park.

One Sunday stands out in my memory. Ada, with her eyes sparkling with excitement, requested a board game. As we rummaged through our toy chest, she found a classic—the Mouse Trap board game. Memories flooded back as I recalled the joy I felt playing this game as a child.

At that moment, without screens or distractions, Ada and I sat down together. The box was opened, and the pieces were laid out before us. With the rulebook as our guide, we constructed the intricate mouse trap. Laughter filled the room as we navigated the twists and turns of the game board, Ada eagerly asking questions and eagerly placing pieces under my guidance.

The time we spent together, the things I taught her, and the way I allowed her to place the pieces and take her time, so the pieces did not break, were so rewarding to her. When we were done, we separated the pieces and placed them in the box. I praised her for helping clean up before we decided to do something else.

Ada went home and told her mom what a wonderful time she had. She explained how we played the game and expressed her pride in her performance.

Reflecting on our afternoon, I realized that these moments held a more profound significance beyond the fun and laughter. They built blocks, nurturing Ada's confidence and self-esteem in subtle yet profound ways. Through our shared experiences, I was her Mimi and mentor, guiding her through self-discovery and growth.

In a world consumed by busyness, these moments of connection truly matter. Whether it's playing board games, exploring nature, or simply sharing a cup of tea and conversation, it is the quality of our presence that leaves a lasting impression on those we hold dear.

As I watch Ada grow and flourish, I'm reminded of the invaluable lessons passed down from my grandmother. In her warmth and wisdom, I found strength and guidance, shaping the person I am today. And now, as I walk alongside Ada on her journey, I am grateful for the opportunity to nurture her confidence and resilience, one meaningful moment at a time.

Ultimately, it's not just about the games we play or the activities we engage in; it is about the bonds we forge and the memories we create. In these moments of connection lies the true essence of love and belonging. We are building future self-confident leaders for tomorrow.

***

Turning Confidence Inside Out

If you met my son, Aaron, you would understand what I mean by turning confidence inside out. In 2017, he wrote a children's book titled "A Moose with a Uke." It's a delightful story for children aged three to ten about Monty the Moose, who finds a ukulele and other instruments floating in a river and shares them with his forest friends. The book includes a song at the end and a coloring book with additional songs.

Aaron decided to share his book at the local library, where the fun began. Today, he performs in libraries, schools, and senior centers throughout New England. During his performances, he reads the story, teaches children how to draw the characters, and plays the ukulele. The kids adore him. He's like the Pied Piper, posting their artwork on Facebook and cheering them on. He builds confidence in children, allowing them to see how wonderful art and music can be.

Our children need to grow their imaginations at a young age, and my son's mission is to inspire that creativity and build confidence. This year, he introduced a new show with a backdrop and a Monty the Moose puppet. Monty talks to the kids, and Aaron has them sing and dance. He even brings them up on stage to sing, draw, and play the ukulele, with everyone clapping and cheering them on.

I am amazed at how my son has shared his talents for writing, drawing, and singing with so many children in his community. His performances are extraordinary, and the children love being with him. We talk almost daily about all the new projects he's working on.

Isn't it amazing how someone can inspire others to be confident and how the confidence we give can make us more creative and confident about our next life's adventure?

When was the last time you looked at confidence this way? Helping others can, in turn, help ourselves.

***

I met Deena a brief time ago; we talked about my book and the many aspects of building confidence. After a conversation, I asked her if she would author a story about her amazing son to bring hope to others facing challenging situations with a loved one.

The Power of Confidence:
Seth's Soaring Journey
Deena Capron

Confidence isn't just about believing in oneself; it's about overcoming challenges, embracing uniqueness, and finding strength in adversity. This is the story of Seth, a remarkable young man whose journey from a struggling, misunderstood child to a confident, accomplished adult is a testament to the incredible power of resilience and determination.

Seth arrived three weeks and five days early, weighing seven pounds one ounce. From the start, he was a very unhappy baby, crying inconsolably for the first nine months. He didn't want to be held or seem to like anyone. Today, we recognize these signs as early indicators of being on the autism spectrum, but in 2001, we were unaware.

At just a few months old, we worried he might be deaf. No matter how loud the noise, he wouldn't react. He ignored us. Every milestone was a struggle, especially potty training. Seth preferred to find a corner rather than be bothered with it.

His teacher couldn't get him to participate productively two weeks into kindergarten. So we visited the pediatrician. At five years old, Seth was diagnosed with ADHD. The medication made an immediate difference. His teacher called me in tears at lunchtime, thrilled that he stayed in his seat, learned, and interacted with his classmates. Praise the Lord!

We managed well until middle school, which was a challenging time. We returned to the pediatrician, who assured us that Seth would achieve great things. We just had to help him get there. At eleven, a specialist diagnosed Seth with Asperger's syndrome.

The school remained difficult. Panic attacks often sent us to the ER, usually over spelling words. Even as a college graduate, Seth still struggles with spelling. Bullying was frequent, as he always carried a Bible and an encyclopedia on WWII tanks. It's not surprising that others found this unusual.

In seventh grade, a new counselor named Stephanie joined us, saving my sanity. She taught us coping skills and how to make task lists and connected us with a life skills coach. Seth began to learn how to integrate into society.

At fifteen, he attended Aviation Camp at Vincennes University and discovered a passion for flying. By the end of the summer, he had earned his private pilot's license! He then joined the Robotics Club, where supportive teachers recognized his intelligence and helped him gain confidence. They appointed him a safety officer, putting his OCD to good use.

His guidance counselor, experienced with autistic students, directed him to a trade school. Seth didn't want to spend four more years in a traditional classroom, so he returned to Vincennes University, making the dean's list every semester in aviation technology.

Now, at twenty-two, Seth lives independently, operates heavy machinery at one of the largest quarries in the US, and recently bought his first new car—all on his own.

It took a village, much love, patience, and prayer. We never accepted limitations or labels. Seth is his own success story, but he's my success story.

Seth's achievements exemplify what confidence, perseverance, and a refusal to accept limitations can accomplish. His journey is a story that inspires and reminds us that anything is possible with confidence and support.

CHAPTER 7

The Power of Self-Esteem

Stand in your power. If you don't feel powerful,
be willing to let someone breathe it into you.

I crossed paths with a business professional during a women's conference five years ago. She consistently sets ambitious goals for herself, both personally and professionally. We discussed my new book and the story you are about to read. Her story is a good example of how her faith nurtures and sustains her confidence.

A Tale of Faith, Transition, and Rebuilding

I was promoted to a senior level of management, and less than one year after my promotion, the individual who hired me was no longer with the firm. It became apparent that my new boss and I were incompatible in a short period.

In addition, I questioned some of their motives in a particular situation and was politely asked to mind my own business. Hence, it was no surprise when I was not offered a position to stay with the new management team. My morale was utterly crushed when I was not offered the job.

I had never been in that situation before, and the high levels of doubt, fear, and anxiety that came over me were almost crippling. I had considered bowing out of management for a few years to be at home with my family.

As such, and after many prayers, I decided to gracefully leave management, relocate my family, and enter a junior position to restart my career. I was allowed to move my family back to my parents' hometown, where I started to rebuild.

During my last week in my former management position, I was saying goodbye to some colleagues, and one of them pulled me aside and asked if he could talk with me privately.

I had never been close to this individual, so I was curious about his parting words. He sat me down and said, "I've been watching how well you've handled this transition, and I'd like to tell you a story about my son."

He told me his faith was essential to him and then shared that he had taken his young son to his first basketball game a few weeks prior. His child's favorite toy was Thomas the Train, and when the family got to the arena and parked the car, they took Thomas the Train away from the child so they wouldn't lose it during the game. His son screamed, cried, and threw a fit in the parking lot.

My colleague said that for a brief moment, he thought this must be what it is like to be God. He emphatically stated he did not mean that to be blasphemous at all.

Instead, he knew that Thomas the Train would be nothing to him if he could just put his son into the arena. His son was about to see bright lights, watch the players, smell the popcorn, and hear the crowd, and at that point, Thomas the Train would become trivial.

He said that's probably how God looks at us sometimes when He knows that what is on the other side of the arena is much better for us, yet we stay focused on Thomas the Train.

My colleague said that having watched me make this transition, I reminded him of that story. He thought that the opportunity for me to restart my career closer to the family could be an event similar to his son's experience at his first basketball game.

That piece of encouragement and that story will stick with me all the days of my life, mainly because he was right.

Rebuilding my career has been a special blessing, and I will forever be grateful.

Faith and confidence work in mysterious ways.

***

Leading with Heart: Confidence and Influence

I met Debra Mainolfi, a dynamic and insightful woman, almost twenty-three years ago. I couldn't author this book without including a story about her and the confidence she inspires in those she believes in.

We first crossed paths at an event showcasing before-and-after photos, filled with laughter and makeovers. By the end of the evening, I invited her to a Mary Kay Cosmetics business meeting. She attended, and we immediately hit it off. Shortly after, she signed up to become a Mary Kay consultant. Although Debra was a successful financial planner, she saw our fun and joined part-time, adding sparkle to her life by selling Mary Kay.

Debra is our glamour gal, passionate about sparkle. Mary Kay offers fun, glitz, and glamour, along with the opportunity to earn extra income. We worked diligently together, and she became one of my first directors on the team. With her help and the support of others, I earned my first pink Cadillac.

Debra instilled belief in me when I thought achieving our goals was impossible. We attended conferences together and mentored many others. After my husband and his brother sold their wire business, we moved to Illinois, and life changed.

Debra transitioned to become a successful bank branch manager. She elevated the branch by utilizing her skills, fantastic personality, and talents, winning numerous awards. Her employees admire and love her, and her clients always feel welcome. She confidently leads and encourages employees to "make your day count."

One day, an employee from another bank spoke to Debra about a job at her branch. This bilingual woman struggled with language and confidence, was not treated well, and was looked over in her previous position. Debra hired her and has mentored her, helping her climb the ladder. This woman is the head teller and aspires to run a bank branch one day. Debra is also a role model in cold-calling, demonstrating to her employees and others how to build relationships. She has brought several women into the banking business, creating self-assurance and confidence.

Beyond banking, Debra has made significant contributions to

the community, helping women and businesses. She mentors many on boards, teaching them how to build a team and work successfully in the community. She always looks to make a difference and prides herself on "being the best you can be."

Confidence is so much more than building ourselves; it is about bringing out the best qualities in others. This not only gives them self-assurance but also enhances our best qualities, ultimately creating our confidence as well.

Confidence Builders

Dream big!

Reflect

EXERCISE

Be grateful

STAND TALL

List your best Qualities

SMILE

Love Fiercely

Stop procrastinating

Pamper yourself

Be OK with failure

Do something new

Read a great book

SAY NO

Think positively

STAND UP FOR YOURSELF

Are you a participant or a spectator?

***

Upon meeting Jennie, her heart of gold shines through effortlessly, embracing all with her radiant personality and warm smile. Though filled with initial hesitations and uncertainties, embarking on the Quiltmaker Café venture reflects a boldness to embrace risks. This leap of faith demands a profound self-assurance and unwavering belief in the envisioned path.

Beyond the Plate: The Power of Community
Jennie Knowlton

The first time I visited a Pay-What-You-Can café was in 2015 during a mother-daughter road trip. My daughter, Elizabeth, had just graduated high school and was about to start her education at Appalachian State University. Although we had raised her to be strong, independent, and resourceful, we knew it would be hard not to see her every day in person, so we set out on a ten-day journey up the East Coast.

My favorite part of that trip will always be the drive time. We spent hours and hours talking about every topic imaginable. It was a bucket list type of trip, and we did everything from Broadway, the Baltimore Aquarium, and the Liberty Bell to the Jersey Shore. But one of the most impressive stops was the Soul Kitchen, a Pay-What-You-Can in Red Bank, New Jersey. The Soul Kitchen is an upscale PWYC. They serve dinner at two timed seatings daily and have an entire staff of volunteers. But the feeling we got while sitting there—sharing a community table with other guests, chatting about how we got there and where we were from—was amazing. It was clear that some guests were regulars, having their only hot meal of the day, but there was no separation of guests. We all sat at the same table, with the same menu, and received the same dignified treatment.

Our trip eventually ended, and Elizabeth went off to Appalachian State. Coincidentally, the home of ASU, Boone, North Carolina, also has a PWYC café downtown. Although the model was similar, the operations were quite different. F.A.R.M. Café in Boone (the letters stand for Feed All Regardless of Means) served its meals in a cafeteria style and used an old pharmacy counter as its community table. Still, the atmosphere at both was welcoming and dignified. It's interesting to think about now. There were only a handful of PWYC cafés open during that time. What is the likelihood that we will visit two within a few months? Life went on, and when my husband, David, and I would visit her at school, we did our best to dine at F.A.R.M. Café to support the local community. Elizabeth even completed some of her required volunteer hours at the café.

In 2019, Elizabeth graduated from ASU and headed off into the world. But as we all know, COVID started less than a year later, and like so many others, we unexpectedly had her back home. As a family, we watched the hardships that struggling families had to endure from afar. The need for more resources. The fear of the unknown.

About a year into COVID, when it was apparent that it was not stopping any time soon, the three of us started conversing about what *we* could do to make a difference.

None of us were in the medical field, but we did our best to stop the spread; we also donated to charities and volunteered at the local food bank. But what *more* could we do? And what could bring joy and meaning to our lives at the same time? What could we do *as a family*?

Then, in December 2020, during one of these discussions, Elizabeth jokingly said we should start a restaurant. We always welcomed her friends over (before COVID) with more than enough food, and we always hosted our family's holidays. David and I immediately, in unison, responded, "Absolutely not!" Restaurants are backbreaking work for little or no pay. And besides, I *hate* cooking!

But then she said, "It could be a Pay-What-You-Can." And that changed everything. We could do that! Wait, could we do that? Yes, we could. Can we do that?

Fortunately, we had some old textbooks about nonprofits to help answer some of our first and biggest questions. Since I was working from home, I had a flexible schedule to start attending webinars and workshops online about the process. After some research, I found an international organization for PWYC cafés that just happened to be holding its virtual conference in January. We decided that the $250 attendance fee was worth the risk! The conference finalized it for us, which was precisely what we sought. That is the story of my own road trip to the Quiltmaker Café. Quote maker? Quiltmaker? What do quilts have to do with cheeseburgers and scrambled eggs? No, we won't be making or selling quilts. And no, I do not quilt myself, although I respect the craft. So why the name for our PWYC?

A children's book inspired the name of the café, which Elizabeth brought home to us in kindergarten. She chose it off the library cart, and my guess would be because of the beautiful, colorful artwork. This book came home to us and became a family favorite bedtime story. *The Quiltmaker's Gift* is about a quiltmaker who makes the most beautiful quilts but only gives them to those in need. A greedy king demands that the quiltmaker give him one, that it will finally be the one thing that brings him happiness. At first, she refuses but eventually agrees to make the king his quilt by adding a single quilt square each time he gives away one of his treasures. When the king finally gives the last of his treasures away, and his quilt is finished, he claims, "I may look poor, but in truth, my heart is full to bursting, filled with memories of all the happiness I've given and received. I'm the richest man I know." Together, they spend their days making and delivering quilts to others. To this day, after reading this story hundreds of times to my daughter and several nieces and nephews, I still get choked up by the powerful ending of this book.

Having struggled with food insecurity at many separate times in my life—as a child, a teenager, a young adult first out on my own, and a young mother with a new baby—I know firsthand what it means to have an empty pantry, anxiously waiting for the next payday.

It can happen to anyone at any time, and it happens to working families, people struggling with addiction, and those needing expensive medical care. And yes, government programs, food banks, and soup kitchens are necessary and helpful. But a PWYC café brings community and dignity into the equation, making it different from a handout. It is a hand-up, an equalizer, a community effort where everyone has value and worth.

This has been, by far, the most challenging job I have *ever* had. I have had to leave my introverted comfort zone and work with other nonprofits, restaurants, government officials, donors, and volunteers. I have had to make speeches, do radio interviews, and be quoted in the newspaper—all things I had happily avoided *my entire life*. I have had to trust, depend, and rely on others when I usually only count on myself. It has been the most challenging job and, amazingly, also the most incredible. I have seen support and encouragement from strangers through donations, time, and friendship. Some days, this all seems too much, and we will never get the doors open and keep them open. But *every* day, I am astounded by this community's generosity and commitment to its fellow members.

The story outlined above reflects a journey of personal growth and empowerment deeply intertwined with the theme of confidence. Here's how:

- stepping out of comfort zones
- taking risks
- overcoming insecurities
- embracing vulnerability
- seeing impact and growth

Despite the challenges faced along the way, the narrator reflects on the incredible journey they have embarked upon and the positive impact it's had on themselves and their community. This reflection underscores a sense of pride and confidence in their ability to effect meaningful change.

In summary, the story is a testament to the transformative power of confidence—how it enables individuals to overcome obstacles, take risks, embrace vulnerability, and make a difference in the world around them.

CHAPTER 8

Feel the Love

Jennifer has elevated her ability in dog handling by establishing a stunning new boarding and grooming facility. The warmth of her welcoming smile instantly makes you feel valued. Her journey exemplifies how the encouragement of others can ignite our own beliefs, showing that confidence isn't just in oneself but influenced by the supportive individuals in our lives.

Loving Connection
Jennifer Miller Farias

Confidence is a feeling of success now. For most people, it grows stronger or fades depending on how one's circumstances change. However, other personality traits also drive one's confidence.

My confidence is driven primarily by my insecurities and fear of failure.

I remember being an eight-year-old child who was very shy and hardly spoke to new people. That was the age I was when I attended my first dog show with my mom. She was supposed to show our shih tzu puppy, but the puppy behaved very poorly. I told her I wanted to show her next time, and she happily allowed me to do so. I remember feeling safe and comfortable as long as I had my dog. Still, to this day, if I feel uncomfortable or down at all, a puppy snuggle gives me the confidence and drive to tackle whatever life sends me.

As time went on, showing dogs made me increasingly confident.

The more successful I became in the dog show ring, the more confident I became in all areas of my life. It wasn't just because of winning or losing. There were positive comments from judges and competitors. More importantly, it was the ability to take a dog that was scared or didn't want to put its tail up and make it happy and confident. This is what always made me feel the best. The dogs that were a challenge or my mentors couldn't get to show them were the dogs that drove me to be more confident. Even today, my most proud moment is when I can turn a scared dog into a beautiful show dog with lots of confidence.

One of my fondest memories that made me feel the most confident is when I was sixteen. I was at the Shih Tzu National Specialty with my mom and mentor, Eileen Nicolas (a.k.a. my "dog show mom"). I was showing a judge (Jacqueline Stacy) whom I admired and who had given me so much advice over the years. This judge pulled my dog and me out of the ring for her final judgment.

I looked up, and she had also pulled out my mentor, who was showing a dog bred by yet another mentor whom I admire very much. I won and became the youngest handler to win the Shih Tzu National

Specialty, and I accomplished that with a dog that had my heart.

It wasn't just about the win.

I got to do it with Eileen by my side, and I knew she would fight back hard to ensure I was doing my best work in the ring. This shows that confidence isn't just in oneself but has much to do with the people around you. I always feel like if my mom is with me, I can do anything because she has always supported every crazy idea I came up with. She has always been by my side, helping me achieve my dreams.

Surrounding yourself with positive people who show confidence in you nurtures your confidence.

***

From Father to Daughter: The Continuing Legacy of a Timepiece

The people passing through our lives have given us wisdom and encouragement to listen to. Not the naysayers, gossipers, and dream stealers. *You* are simply the best if you believe it. If not, find someone who will breathe the belief into you.

About six months ago, I was having coffee with a mortgage broker. Kelly had been in the business for several years and had remarkable success. As we sat there drinking our coffee, I commented about the beautiful watch she had on her wrist. It had a large face with beautiful numerals. The band was gold but not lavish.

She said it had been her father's, and he had earned it for being the number one salesperson in his company.

She went on to tell me that when her father passed away, she asked her mother for the watch. Kelly's mom was so pleased that she wanted it and offered to have it cleaned and polished. Kelly said, "No, Mom, I want it just how it is to remember Dad." Kelly then told me she wore the watch every time she had a big sale to close.

She told me today was the day, so she wore the watch. It was a significant builder deal, and she needed the wristwatch to remind her that she could accomplish this sale.

A few days later, I called her to see how the sale went, and she told me the confidence she felt knowing her dad was right there on her wrist helped her gain the sale.

Through Kelly's experience, we are reminded of the importance of surrounding ourselves with positivity and encouragement and listening to the voices of wisdom and belief that uplift us. In a world often filled with naysayers and dream stealers, the unwavering support of loved ones and cherished mementos can propel us toward our goals.

Indeed, the power of cherished heirlooms goes beyond their physical presence; they carry the memories, values, and encouragement of those who came before us, empowering us to face daunting tasks with determination and conviction.

Kelly's story poignantly reminds us of that belief in oneself, fostered by others' belief, can be a powerful force for success and fulfillment. If doubt creeps in, seeking out, as Kelly did, those who breathe belief into us can reignite our confidence and our path to greatness.

***

The Confidence Blueprint: Building Success through Helping Others Succeed

Sitting here today, I realize why this book is so important. Today was a long but enriching day. I have met with several different clients, not just in meetings but also in good conversations. Most of my assistance in these conversations entailed listening to and understanding my clients' needs. My cup is full when I can help someone through a situation and find the keys to open the door. My confidence gives them a feeling of value.

After an employee's traumatic departure, one of my clients needed to make a Zoom call with the other employees to explain the situation. I knew she felt challenged by this. We discussed it, and I realized she needed to keep it positive and on point and make the employees feel important. I said, "Start with an agenda. This way, you feel in control and lead with compassion."

After the call, she told me it went very well. She also said that keeping the employees in the loop every couple of weeks would keep her in tune with the team.

Age brings wisdom; today, considering all the noise and lack of time we constantly deal with, my job is to dig deep and find solutions to inspire the people I work with.

I have a gift. I build connections, open doors, and listen closely to my clients' needs. Coaching is so much more than goal setting and strategy. It is the ability to inspire and give help. My daughter calls me the "proactive starter."

The other evening, I was at a networking meeting, conversing with a young man who has opened several dry-cleaning operations and drop-off centers.

He said the business was doing well but needed to capture higher-end clients. We talked more about him opening another drop-off in our growing community. "Have you considered being known as the concierge?" I asked him. I said, "Go into law offices, Realtors, insurance, and other businesses where they wear suits and dress shirts." This idea—doing pickup at different offices on certain days—had never occurred to him. He has since hired me, and we are now developing a plan of action.

What does this have to do with confidence? Sometimes confidence comes not just from what you can do but precisely what you can do for others.

My ability to assist others with vision and listening and connect my clients to those who can help build and develop their businesses has increased my confidence tenfold.

When we can be more for others, we breathe confidence into them; we inspire them to think more clearly and lead better. I see myself as a resource. I always ask, "Where are you challenged right now? Where can I best strategize with you?"

This talent has been given to me to inspire others, and I have developed it with lots of practice. Arnold Palmer reportedly said, "The more I practice, the luckier I get." How true this is!

What gifts have you been given that you can offer to others? Communication is the key that opens the door and breathes confidence into others.

***

The Power of Friendship: Finding Confidence through Loss

Confidence is a universal struggle, something we all grapple with from time to time. Despite our desire to feel assured, those whispers of self-doubt often surface when we step out of our comfort zones, take risks, or embrace new experiences.

Cultivating confidence is the cornerstone of healthy self-esteem and personal growth, yet it remains challenging for many.

Self-confidence is indeed a superpower.

Once you begin to believe in yourself, the magic unfolds. After years of ups and downs, I finally realized I needed to stop chasing my dreams. I needed to stop doubting myself and instead focus on helping others find what they wanted, knowing that my dreams would become reality. I also realized that confiding in others, being open to their opinions, listening, and pivoting when needed were essential. It was a lesson in humility and growth.

I will never forget meeting Sandi. She applied for a job I posted in my insurance agency, possessing the bookkeeping skills I sought. She was there for me when I merged my agency, witnessing both the successes and the failures. Sandi was a pillar of support through thick and thin. Our friendship blossomed into a sisterhood, and she was there for me when my father passed away. She had a way of setting me straight, of believing in me even when I was at my lowest. Sandi acknowledged my strengths, and when I shared my plan to start a new Mary Kay business, she was the first to cheer me on. I needed a fresh start, and I was scared.

Friends like Sandi are rare gems. Life took its course, and I remarried and moved to Massachusetts. She, too, had her challenges, eventually moving back home to Pittsburgh after her husband passed away. Despite the distance, we kept in touch. Our conversations were like picking up right where we left off, as if no time had passed.

In January 2016, I called Sandi. We spoke for about an hour, reminiscing about old times and catching up on each other's lives. I shared my plans to move to North Carolina and insisted she visit. We laughed, made plans, and she promised to see us once we were settled.

A couple of days later, the phone rang. The caller ID displayed Sandi's name. Excitedly, I answered, "We haven't talked in a while! Ha-ha." There was silence at the other end. "Hello?" I said again. Then a voice, not Sandi's, identified herself as Debbie, Sandi's sister. Her tone was somber. She had some unfortunate news to share—Sandi had passed away suddenly. I was stunned, crushed. This woman who had given me my superpower, who was my beacon of strength and support, was now gone.

To aid you on your journey toward greater confidence, here are eight suggestions to kickstart your progress:

- *Confront your fears.* Fear is often the root cause of low self-confidence. When fear dictates our actions, it amplifies the voice of self-doubt. Confronting your fears head-on, even in small ways, can diminish their power. Recall a past instance where you faced fear, the feeling of liberation and pride that followed. Commit to doing something that scares you regularly to see your confidence flourish.
- *Embrace failure.* Without failure, there can be no true success. Being comfortable with the prospect of failure is crucial for growth. Each failure is a lesson in disguise, offering opportunities for learning and improvement. Accept your mistakes, use them as stepping stones, and propel yourself forward.

- *Challenge your doubts.* Doubt undermines confidence, fostering uncertainty and cynicism. When self-doubt creeps in, question its validity. Challenge the negative beliefs it presents, often finding they lack substantial evidence.
- *Acknowledge your strengths.* Individuals lacking confidence tend to focus on weaknesses rather than strengths. Create a list of your strengths, talents, and achievements. Review this list daily to reinforce positive self-perception. The messages we repeatedly expose ourselves to influence our beliefs greatly.
- *Project confidence.* The adage "fake it till you make it" holds wisdom. To feel more confident, embody confidence. Recall a moment when you felt self-assured, using all senses to recreate that feeling. Posture and attire also play a role; choose postures and clothing that exude confidence, boosting your self-perception.
- *Immerse yourself in empowering media.* Music and motivational content can evoke positive emotions. Surround yourself with uplifting media, whether music that energizes you or motivational videos that inspire. Limit exposure to stressful news and negative influences.
- *Set achievable goals.* Accomplishments significantly affect self-confidence. Commit to realistic goals and follow through with action. By honoring your commitments to yourself, you build trust in your abilities. Start with small, attainable goals and gradually expand from there.
- *Make a positive impact.* Contributing to society through volunteering or charitable donations reminds us of our significance. Small acts of kindness or generosity can uplift others and reinforce your sense of purpose, empowering you and boosting self-confidence.

Embarking on this journey toward greater confidence requires patience and persistence. By consistently implementing these steps, you'll gradually cultivate a more profound belief in yourself and your capabilities, unlocking immense potential.

This story poignantly reminds us of the effect friendships can have on our lives, especially when they believe in us and support us through our journeys of growth and self-discovery.

Dear, sweet Sandi, if she were here today, she would be kicking me in the ass and telling me to get this book finished. Thank you, Sandi. I am listening, confronting my fears, challenging my doubts, and finally publishing it.

***

Believe in yourself and be your kind of beautiful.
—**Peggy Young**

***

Knowing Carol has been a true delight. She exudes care and compassion, and her Reiki treatments work wonders in alleviating pain and stress. Her journey underscores a profound truth: achieving peak confidence is impossible when burdened by stress. Carol's wisdom echoes, "To nurture your life, you must first nurture yourself."

Harmonizing Healing: A Nurse's Journey into Holistic Wellness
Carol Zackman

Carol's career in nursing spans over forty-two years, beginning in the fast-paced realm of neonatal care. The demands of this intense environment took a toll, manifesting stress-related ailments. Seeking holistic remedies, Carol discovered Reiki, an ancient Japanese healing art centered on energy manipulation for stress relief and healing. Embracing Reiki, she seamlessly integrated it into her nursing practice, witnessing its transformative effects on herself and her patients.

In my early years, I worked as a neonatal nurse and nurse practitioner. This very fast-paced, intense job caused me a lot of stress. Besides working twenty-four-hour shifts, I performed spinal taps and inserted breathing tubes, arterial lines, and chest tubes into babies weighing between two and ten pounds.

When they were placed into my hands at birth, I would "turn on my Reiki hands" while I dried them off. Most infants would turn and look me right in the eyes once they felt the energy. I also used it on sick infants.

One baby was unable to suck on a bottle. An emergency C-section delivered him after the uterus ruptured during labor. He was without oxygen for a short while and had also hemorrhaged. His mother had been bringing mud from Macedonia, water from Lourdes, and many prayer cards that she put in his incubator. I asked his mother about giving him treatment with Reiki. Once I explained what it was, she agreed.

The treatment was done just before his next feeding. I handed her the bottle, and he drained it! I don't know who cried harder, me or the mother.

Many nurses began asking me for treatment whenever they had headaches or were stressed. Some would jokingly ask me to keep my hands on their shoulders all day to keep them calm and prevent stressful headaches.

My holistic journey expanded to include essential oils, notably peppermint and lavender, which I found invaluable in alleviating discomfort and promoting relaxation, particularly among expectant mothers. Observing the profound impact of holistic approaches compared to traditional symptom-centric treatments, I ventured into CBD products and herbal remedies, addressing root causes rather than merely alleviating symptoms. Why didn't the medical community use these products instead of treating symptoms?

Meditation became another cornerstone of my stress-management toolkit, providing profound benefits during challenging life transitions. Guided by my yoga instructor, she mastered breathing techniques that effectively dissipated tension, fostering a profound mind-body connection.

When you are stressed, have you ever noticed how your body feels? You only breathe with the upper lobes of your lungs, bring your shoulders closer to your ears, and clench your jaw and gut. My yoga instructor began teaching me breathing techniques to help me handle stress. It is impossible to continue to hold my body so tightly when I breathe deeply or in certain patterns.

Continuing my quest for holistic wellness, I delved into mind-body practices, such as Holy Fire Reiki, which harnesses internal healing energies. Through these techniques, I facilitate transformative healing experiences and witness remarkable shifts in my clients.

In addition to Reiki and meditation, I embrace a multifaceted approach to stress reduction, incorporating yoga, exercise, time management, social support, self-care, and a wholesome diet into my lifestyle. With these holistic practices at my disposal, stress no longer holds sway over my life, empowering me to navigate challenges with resilience and grace.

Through her journey, Carol learns that true confidence stems from external achievements, inner balance, and resilience. By addressing stress at its core and embracing holistic practices, she cultivates a profound trust in her ability to navigate life's challenges with grace and poise. This newfound confidence radiates from within, empowering Carol to face adversity with courage and conviction.

How do you navigate challenges? What holistic practices would help and empower you and give you the confidence to move forward?

CHAPTER 9

Change

The Young Eagle
Tom Reilly

The next of young eagles hung on every word as the master eagle described his exploits. This was an important day for the eaglets. They were preparing for their first solo flight from the nest. It was the confidence builder many of them needed to fulfill their destiny.

"How far can I travel?" asked one of the eaglets.

"How far can you see?" responded the master eagle.

"How high can I fly?" quizzed the young eagle.

"How far can you stretch your wings?" asked the old eagle.

"How long can I fly?" the eaglet persisted.

"How far is the horizon?" the mentor rebounded.

"How much should I dream?" asked the eaglet.

"How much can you dream?" The older, wiser eagle smiled.

"How much can I achieve?" the young one continued.

"How much can you believe?" the old eagle challenged.

Frustrated by the banter, the young eagle demanded, "Why don't you answer my questions?"

"I did."

"Yes, but you answered them with questions."

"I answered them the best I could."

"But you're the master eagle. You're supposed to know everything. If you can't answer these questions, who can?"

"You," the old, wise eagle reassured.

"Me? How?" the young eagle was confused.

"No one can tell you how high to fly or how much to dream. It's different for each eagle.

Only you and God know how far you'll go. No one on this earth knows your potential or what's in your heart. You alone will answer that. The only thing that limits you is the edge of your imagination."

The young eagle, puzzled by this, asked, "What should I do?"

"Look to the horizon, spread your wings, and fly."

***

The Power of Color and Its Ability to Enhance Confidence

I have always been intrigued by the way colors can influence our mood. Colors have a profound effect on our emotions and perspectives. They play a crucial role in shaping our self-image and perception of others. When it comes to confidence, colors hold considerable sway, capable of boosting our self-belief and nurturing a sense of empowerment.

Fashion and interior design have always fascinated me. I had hoped to pursue a design education, but it was not meant to be. Looking back on my journey, I realize color's significant impact on our everyday lives. Dressing to exude confidence brings me happiness and instills a sense of empowerment.

Color acts as your cheerleader, infusing each step with pep and sass. It's the supportive companion to your inner superhero, whispering, "You've got this!" in every shade. So why settle for blending in when you can dazzle the world with your vibrant personality? Embrace the rainbow and watch your confidence soar higher than ever!

What is your favorite color? Mine is purple—it exudes elegance every time I wear it.

Here is a glimpse into the significance of various colors:

Red commands attention with its boldness and vitality, often associated with strength and passion. Whether it's a striking red ensemble or daring lipstick, this color radiates confidence, making a powerful statement wherever you go.

Blue, with its calming and trustworthy aura, exudes professionalism and reliability. Whether a tailored suit or a chic dress, wearing blue enhances self-assurance, ensuring you feel capable and composed.

Yellow symbolizes optimism and energy, evoking a sense of joy and positivity. It uplifts spirits and radiates confidence to those around you.

Purple, historically linked to royalty, exudes luxury and creativity, signaling introspection and refinement.

Green embodies freshness and healing, rooted in its connection to nature, offering stability and rejuvenation.

Orange blends strength and cheerfulness, conveying confidence, sociability, and enthusiasm.

Black epitomizes sophistication and elegance, imparting poise and polish for formal occasions or important meetings.

Choosing colors that resonate with you is pivotal in harnessing their confidence-boosting potential. Whether it's the boldness of red, the calm of blue, the joy of yellow, the luxury of purple, the healing of green, the cheer of orange, or the timeless elegance of black, embracing colors that make you feel good significantly impacts your demeanor and interactions.

Beyond clothing, surrounding yourself with confidence-inspiring colors in your environment can positively influence your mindset.

Whether through room decor or colorful stationery, the right hues create spaces conducive to productivity and self-assurance.

Colors transcend mere aesthetics; they possess the power to shape our moods and mindsets. Embrace the hues that empower you, whether in your attire or surroundings, and let confidence become your guiding force.

Color can be the confidence boost your wardrobe needs! Imagine striding into a bold red or vibrant yellow room. Suddenly, you are not just wearing clothes; you are wearing attitude. Your outfit becomes your hype squad, cheering you on with every step. So, next time you are feeling down, throw on some color and let your confidence radiate.

Change is hard at first,
Messy in the middle,
Gorgeous at the end.
—Robin Sharma

***

Lessons I Learned about Building Confidence

Throughout my life journey, I have encountered individuals facing challenges far more significant than my own. We each experience highs and lows, and how we navigate these moments shapes our confidence and character. Here are my top ten suggestions for cultivating confidence:

1. Embrace your uniqueness. Avoid comparing yourself to others; you are meant to be the best version of yourself.
2. Let go of concerns about what you cannot control.
3. You can learn more from today than dwelling in the past.
4. Stay humble; there's endless knowledge to gain.
5. Don't hesitate to ask questions; it shows respect and makes others feel valued.
6. Step out of your comfort zone; growth happens when you challenge yourself.
7. Extend kindness daily; it boosts your confidence and brightens someone's day.
8. Focus on your goals and the vision of what you want to achieve.
9. Share your smile generously; you never know who might need it.
10. Remember, your destiny is in your hands.

***

Change the way you think
to change the way you feel.
—Robin Roberts

***

Empowering Excellence: An Inspiring Journey

About a year ago, I had the privilege of meeting an extraordinary woman. It happened during a Professional Women's business gathering, and her infectious smile and genuine warmth immediately drew me in. Intrigued, I resolved to connect with her further, and after swapping business cards, we scheduled a meeting at her office for the following week.

Claire is an exceptionally modest individual with an impressive background. She attended Phillips Academy Andover, the Naval Academy, and Cornell University. Alongside her academic pursuits, Claire distinguished herself as a collegiate athlete and devoted coach to young rowers. While she's trained varsity and elite athletes, her passion for coaching novices truly shines. In months, those who once doubted their athletic abilities and felt apprehensive about a new sport transformed into dedicated and knowledgeable rowers under Claire's guidance.

Beyond her coaching commitments, Claire's life revolves around her marriage to Zach and their beautiful daughter. Their dream of owning a construction company materialized in March 2020 when they boldly embarked on entrepreneurship.

Despite grappling with seven cancer diagnoses, including brain, thyroid, and breast cancer (with the second brain tumor removed in March 2020), Claire's enthusiasm never wavered. Not even starting a construction company amid a new brain cancer diagnosis during the COVID crisis seemed to deter her.

Getting to know Claire was an absolute delight. She's an exceptional woman who pours her heart and soul into the employees of the company she and her husband have built. Claire stands as a beacon for those striving for excellence. Through her tireless work ethic and unwavering integrity, she radiates a confidence that uplifts and empowers others. She encourages women to aim for their highest aspirations and embodies empowerment in every facet of her life.

Claire's involvement on the board of Hope Renovations reflects her commitment to empowering women. This organization is dedicated to equipping women with the skills needed for rewarding careers in construction trades. Through hands-on training and renovation projects, they assist older adults in aging comfortably and safely in their homes.

Individuals like Claire have been a constant source of inspiration and strength. They bolster my confidence and impart invaluable wisdom that I'm honored to share with others. These remarkable women teach me that while money isn't everything, it allows us to make choices that benefit our families and enable us to contribute positively to society.

Reflecting on the many individuals who've enriched my life, from my mother, who instilled the values of kindness and resilience, to mentors who imparted the importance of hard work and perseverance, each has left an indelible mark on my journey.

Who has made a difference in your life's journey? Seek out those whose wisdom you can glean and grow alongside.

***

CHAPTER 10

Next Steps

We gain confidence, wisdom,
and inner strength as we age.

Boosting Confidence: Simple Strategies

I am a super-ager, feeling as fine as aged wine and occasionally as frisky as whiskey. But what's the connection to confidence? Society often pushes retirement upon us as we age. Adopting a fresh perspective is crucial, regardless of where we stand in our life's journey.

Here are some key ways so that we can keep revising and renewing the way we look at the world and ourselves:

- *Cultivate meaningful friendships* and surround yourself with positive individuals. Regular communication with these colleagues can bolster confidence.
- *Mindful eating habits* contribute to our well-being not only for ourselves but also for those we cherish and support.
- *Managing stress is paramount.* While stress is ubiquitous, there are essential strategies to minimize its impact. My acquaintance Carol Zackman, RN, specializes in stress-reduction techniques. She teaches breathing exercises and does Reiki to bring the calm we all need.

- *Injecting flair into our attire,* regardless of age, can elevate our confidence and even draw compliments. How does that make you feel?
- *Now, let's talk about hair.* Cut, color, and add more, but get the hair in order! When was the last time you received a compliment?
- *Music is the heart and soul of confidence.* Something upbeat or soothing, whatever you like, will make you feel better. Dance around the room; feel the energy. You deserve the very best.
- *Embrace a positive mindset rooted in gratitude.* Challenge yourself, practice self-affirmations, and document your journey in a journal.
- My mother also said, "If Mama is happy, everyone is happy." *Bring on the happy!*
- *Prioritize self-care.* It's nonnegotiable.

***

Leaving a Legacy

To end this book, I wanted to give you things to consider about how we live and how we can build our confidence for a future beyond ourselves. Building a legacy means creating something you can pass on that will endure through generations.

Why is this important, and what does it have to do with confidence? Everything we do is an example for future generations of our values, manners, beliefs, and traditions. We pass them down from generation to generation. The good and the bad are all that we leave behind.

We make memories, lead by example, and show the world what makes us different and what we do best.

Please consider how you will leave your legacy and instill belief in this next generation. No matter your age, you can start this process now. We need to live by example. We can always tell our children to be honest, kind, hardworking, and trustworthy, but we need to show them the way through the circumstances we encounter. Based on their life experiences and how they handle situations, they will learn to overcome obstacles, stand up for themselves, and be compassionate.

Are we approaching each day with gratitude?

We should not boast about our accomplishments but be grateful for all we have. Are we giving others our wisdom, kindness, and generosity? Let's strive to do our best; when we fail, get up and try again. Absolute failure is never trying.

I saw this by Jane Fonda (yes, I go back to the exercise queen I mentioned earlier in this book. I admire her because she is a trailblazer). Fonda admits she doesn't think much about her legacy. "I'm not scared of dying. I think I'm telling the truth when I say that," Fonda says. "But I am terrified of getting to the end with many regrets when it's too late to do anything. And when you figure that out, it instructs how you live between now and the end."

I feel the same. I have so much to do, and the clock is ticking like a time bomb. First and foremost, I love being with my family and grandkids, writing, playing the ukulele, watercolor painting, speaking, working, and anything new to fill my time.

In a prior story, Judy discussed journaling and how it can provide guidance and comfort. Writing is a choice. I write when I need to clear my mind or tell one of my grandchildren something we did together to create a memory or how proud I am of their accomplishments.

Here is something fun for me over the years. "Grammie mail." I love to send mail when they least expect it—a card, something silly,

I am proud of you, or you can do it mail. The smiles and calls are priceless. We all like to receive a little sunshine.

Ultimately, leaving a meaningful legacy is personal. It often involves a combination of personal values, passions, and the desire to affect the world positively. Individuals may strive to leave a legacy that reflects their principles, ideals, and the mark they want to make on the earth for future generations.

***

It's not how long we live; it's how we live that counts.
—Charles Osgood

***

Poem: Courage + Action = Confidence

It's a glorious morning, but I hide my head.
Don't know what the day may bring.
"Wait!" I say. "Get out of bed!"
"Get up, get dressed, and do your thing.
Get ready to take on the world and more!"
as I confidently walk out the door.

I hesitate with a sigh, the stress of the
emails piling high,
the traffic, the meetings.
Not even sure what's the right way.
How do I handle myself today?
What was I taught in this book I just read?
Courage + Action = Confidence, it said.
Now I remember as I ponder this thought.
I know how to tackle the day.
With a smile and stride that shows what I've got
"I am worth more!" Hear me say it a lot.

CONTRIBUTORS

Christine Chase
Sacredyounc.com

Christine Chase offers guidance, encouragement, and growth in a nurturing process that allows women to make changes that create balance, empowerment, and joy by cultivating a deeper relationship with themselves.

Claire Coffey, CEO
Intrepid Build
CCoffey@Intrepid-Build.com
Intrepid-Build.com

Claire Coffey is a visionary leader and the driving force behind Intrepid Build. She fosters a collaborative environment with teams at every level of the build and prioritizes the success of skilled trades, bringing a fresh perspective to contractors' responsibility in the industry. She is married to her business partner, Zachary, and they have a beautiful daughter, Jillian.

Joanne Cunneen
Joannepcv@gmail.com

Joanne Cunneen is a retired educator, director of religious education, and pastoral associate in an urban Roman Catholic parish in New York City. She holds master's degrees in early childhood education and Roman Catholic theology.

Aishling Dalton-Kelly, President and CEO
Aishling Care Academy
Aishling@aishlingcareacademy.com
Aishlingcareacademy.com

Aishling Dalton Kelly, the owner of Aishling Companion Home Care for ten years and current owner and operator of Aishling Care Academy, dedicates her life's work to recruiting CNAs who embody genuine compassion for seniors and deliver care with the utmost respect and quality to those who've paved the way for us.

Aurelie Gallagher
Irish Eyes Design
aurelie@irisheyesdesign.com
Irisheyesdesign.com

Aurelie Gallagher is an intuitive graphic designer passionate about creating balanced layouts and connecting ideas. She lives in the northern suburbs of Chicago, enjoys watching her adult children thrive, and endeavors to build her confidence daily through her life and work at Irish Eyes Design.

Jennifer Halloran, PhD, BCPA (board-certified patient advocate)
Everybody Needs A Nurse Patient Advocates
jhalloran@EverybodyNeedsANurse.com
EverybodyNeedsANurse.com

Jennifer Halloran specializes in creative, out-of-the-box strategies that She uses to support the business development of Everybody Needs A Nurse Patient Advocates. She is also involved in developing the field of patient advocacy on a national level through speaking engagements, board memberships, and teaching.

Jessica Harling, Founder, President
Behind the Design
Jessica@gobehindthedesign.com
Gobehindthedesign.com

Jessica Harling founded Behind the Design, a Chicago-based consulting firm, and is a leading expert in people and process development for the interior design industry. They nurture top talent through recruiting, employee training, and streamlining systems that increase productivity and impact the company's bottom line.

Judy Harrelson
Speaker: Holistic Health and Mindful Awareness
Broadway Hemp—Sales Manager
Judysharrelson@gmail.com
Broadwayhemp.com

Judy Harrelson practices and teaches holistic health and mindful awareness. She also offers workshops for manifesting with vision boards. Broadway Hemp, organically grown wellness, is the perfect addition to her natural wellness practice. Judy grew up in England and now lives in North Carolina.

***Sharon Anita Hill*, President**
Sharon Hill International
sharon@sharonhillinternational.com
www.SharonHillInternational.com

Sharon Hill is a certified etiquette expert trained by the American Business Etiquette Trainers Association. Combining her passion for business etiquette, diversity in the workplace, and her MBA research on organizational behavior, Sharon is recognized as an authority on American business etiquette for companies, universities, groups, associations, and individuals.

Jennie Knowlton, Executive Director and Cofounder
The Quiltmaker Cafe
Info@thequiltmakercafe.org
Thequiltmakercafe.org

Jennie Knowlton is excited to see her family's dream come to fruition and is amazed at the support the Chatham community has shown for the Quiltmaker Café. She cofounded this nonprofit with her husband and daughter in 2021. The organization is "pay what you can." There are about forty of these throughout the country. Please see the last page of the book for more information. Proceeds from the book are being donated to the organization for one year.

Leslie Lipps
Power Your Brand
Leslie@leslielipps.com
Leslielipps.com

Leslie is an online marketing professional. Her job is to elevate a website from good to extraordinary by providing strategic and design thinking that only comes from experience. I have worked with Leslie for fifteen years.

Debra Mainolfi, Branch Officer
Freedom Credit Union
Dmainolfi@freedom.coop

Debra Mainolfi prides herself on her work, her customers, and taking care of her employees. She plays a significant role in the community with all her philanthropic work. Debra is a dear friend I have known for twenty-six years. She is married and lives in Western Massachusetts.

Jennifer Miller-Farias
Doggie Dude Ranch
DoggieDudeRanchKennel@gmail.com
DoggieDudeRanchKennel.com

Jennifer Miller Farias began working as a handler and learning how to care for dogs at the highest level of competition. She was taught by some of the best how to keep dogs in the best physical, mental, and emotional health. Today, she and her husband opened in 2024 a dog boarding, grooming, and daycare facility in Pittsboro, North Carolina. She is dedicated to loving and caring for pets. "At the

Doggie Dude Ranch, we enjoy making man's best friend look and feel great in a safe and structured environment."

Sophia Chase Munson
Munson Law Firm, PLLC
Sophia@munsonlawfirmnc.com
Munsonlawfirmnc.com

Sophia Munson is a mother, a lawyer, and an entrepreneur. She and her husband, Mike, run the Munson Law Firm, PLLC, a boutique estate planning and business law firm with offices in Chapel Hill, North Carolina, and Fairfax, Virginia. They have two amazing and stubborn children, Chase and Juliette. Sophia and her family live in Chapel Hill in a messy home with their sweet mutts, Lucy and Rosie.

Tracy Palmatier, RD, LDN
Root Source Health and Wellness
rootsoucehealth@gmail.com
www.rootsourcewellness.com

Tracy Palmatier is a registered dietitian with more than ten years of specialized nutrition expertise. She emphasizes whole-food nutrition and food as medicine. She founded Root Source Health and Wellness, a holistic practice that delves into the interconnected realms of body, mind, and soul.

Tom Reilly, Professional speaker and author
Tom@tomreillyblog.com
Tomreillyblog.com

Tom Reilly wrote *The Young Eagle* (featured in this book), published by Motivation Press. Tom is the author of sixteen books and an editorial contributor to several magazines. Tom is an avid golfer, Harley-Davidson rider, and fountain pen collector. Tom's writings cover many topics: patriotism, war, inspiration, humor, short stories, fiction, nonfiction, and poetry.

Emma Schoch

Emma Schoch will be a first-year student in high school for the 2024–2025 school year. She achieved many accolades in her sixth- to eighth-grade journey. She continues to speak for the Optimist Club and was asked to give the commencement speech at the eighth-grade graduation.

Rachel Thomas
Rachel Thomas Photography
RachelThomaspics@gmail.com
RachelThomasphotography.com

Rachel captures the essence of your story through exquisite fine art photography. Elevating moments and milestones with a thoughtfully curated, high-touch professional experience.

Gigi Verrey
Very Smart Ideas, LLC
Gigi@gigiverrey.com
https://verysmartideas.com

Gigi Verrey is an advocate for limb difference awareness. Born with an upper limb difference, her mission is to help normalize limb difference by showing how to do everyday tasks in the home, kitchen, and garden with one hand. Gigi is a digital creator on social media @

verysmartideas. When not working her day job, Ms. Verrey works as an actor to help bring attention to the need for diversity in the media.

Scott Walker, PhD
Walker Word Smith
Walkerwordsmith@gmail.com

Scott works with subject matter experts and other team members to share complex ideas in clear and compelling language, developing communications strategies that connect readers to ideas and drive organizations toward their goals. Expert editor, writer, and proofreader.

Carol Zackman, RN, MSN
Heart Centered Healing
HeartCenteredRN@gmail.com
HeartCenteredRN.com

Carol Zackman is a master's-prepared nurse with more than forty-three years of experience. She is now a nurse consultant who assists individuals, businesses, and small groups transforming their "Frazzle into Dazzle" by decreasing stress levels using holistic methods.

ACKNOWLEDGMENTS

It takes an extraordinary team to make this dream come true. I am fortunate to have surrounded myself with intelligent, caring individuals who share my vision.

Leslie Lipps, with her diligence, kept the ball rolling. She is so creative, and I love her out-of-the-box thinking. She always says, "Let's get it done. I am here for you."

Scott Walker, PhD, is an experienced, award-winning writer and editor. Scott is a former university English professor and a highly versatile communications professional.

Rachel Thomas captured the images that made the photography come to life. It is always great to work with her.

Aurelie Gallagher stepped up with enthusiasm to develop the beautiful cover art. As an art director at Irish Eyes Design, she used her graphic design to develop what I had in mind.

Thank you to all my family for your support and insight, especially Greg, my husband, who has always supported me. I love you so much. I appreciate your encouragement and patience.

I am grateful for your friendship and support, for those I have not named individually.

Jean MacDonald's book is like receiving a secret map to success from your best friend. Her raw honesty wraps around you like a cozy sweater, instantly boosting your confidence. Jean inspires you to celebrate every step of your journey, from 'oops' moments to triumphant high-fives, reminding you that confidence is built through experience (and a few delightful faceplants). I couldn't put the book down and felt genuinely inspired with each page turn. So grab some popcorn and an open mind—when you reach the last page, you'll feel ready to take action confidently!

Kirstin H.

Friend, Client, and Inspired Reader

Jean's book, "Be Wild, Be Crazy, Be You!" is a testament to her passion for coaching, sharing, and inspiring others. What makes this book truly remarkable are the stories Jean shares and the accounts of the extraordinary women she's encountered along the way—each one navigating her journey of lost and regained confidence.

This book is more than just a collection of stories. It is a guide for anyone seeking to build inner strength, nurture courage, and apply these principles in their own lives to achieve greater confidence. As Jean said, Courage + Action = Confidence. I encourage you to embrace the wisdom within these pages and let it guide you toward personal growth.

GC Crump

Software Engineer / Interior Designer

Jean creates a powerful narrative on the importance of confidence and how embracing it can lead to breaking free from self-induced barriers to success and happiness. "Be Wild, Be Crazy, Be You" is a must-read regardless of your confidence journey.

Jennifer Hedrick, nonprofit leader.

Confidence for a younger woman.

You will make mistakes. Don't look back; yesterday is gone, and tomorrow is ahead. Be grateful for the hard times; without them, you would not grow.

When I met Jean at a speaking engagement, I was at a low point in my life, with low confidence, and had an opportunity to take a role I didn't think I could manage, yet with encouragement and coaching by Jean, I achieved my goal and succeeded. Always surround yourself with positive, encouraging friends, business partners, etc.. don't listen to negative feedback, whether it's your mind or outside influence.

Florica Shepherd, Branch Manager, Loan Depot

Jean MacDonald is a champion for women who claim their strength as they tackle life's hurdles. She has a gift for igniting our internal powers of resilience, and no woman should miss the opportunity to learn from her and the network she surrounds herself with!

Corrine Cottrell, COO, Munson Law Firm

Confidence is a learned attribute. Following Jean's story has allowed me to realize that we each gain confidence differently. With Jean's thoughtful stories, I know I can accomplish anything with the right mindset. Thank you, Jean, for your openness to sharing your experiences so we can all grow.

Elizabeth Mauney, Community Relations Director

ABOUT THE AUTHOR

And one day
she discovered
that she
was fierce,
and strong,
and full of fire,
and that not even she
could hold
herself back
because her
passion burned
brighter than
her fears.
—Mark Anthony

Yes, You Can!

picture of Author **Jean MacDonald**, affectionately known as the "*Queen of Connections*" in high-profile business networking circles, has been a leading figure in leadership, networking, and sales strategy development since 1985. Her expertise has enabled countless clients to enhance their business brands, expand their outreach, and boost their bottom lines.

Jean began her career in the commercial insurance industry, transforming a small business into a multimillion-dollar enterprise representing elite companies nationwide.

Her leadership and business acumen later found a new stage at Mary Kay Cosmetics, where she achieved extraordinary sales volumes and leadership milestones. Jean earned the use of the company's signature cars twelve times, including five of the prestigious pink Cadillac. She was a top producer but also excelled as a top recruiter and trainer, building successful teams across the country.

Currently, Jean owns Business Brewing, where she serves as a communication and business strategist, corporate sales trainer, speaker, and author. She is a certified advisor for How to Fascinate, an assessment tool that helps individuals understand their unique strengths and communication brand.

As a Distinguished Toastmaster, Jean sets ambitious goals both personally and professionally. The Distinguished Toastmaster (DTM) award represents the highest level of educational achievement in Toastmasters

Jean is deeply involved in her community. She founded the Professional Women of Chatham and Orange Counties in North Carolina and actively takes part in Toastmasters International and the Chatham County Chamber of Commerce.

Married to Greg, they live in North Carolina. They have three successful children and enjoy the company of their seven grandchildren. Jean cherishes family time, traveling, beach outings, playing the ukulele, watercolor painting, rowing, and walking their dog.

Jean MacDonald

You have the *power.*
Don't let anyone tell you
differently!
—Jean MacDonald

The **Quiltmaker**
CAFE

Part of the proceeds of this book are being donated to the Quiltmaker Café.

The Quiltmaker Café is a nonprofit organization in Pittsboro, North Carolina, striving to operate as a counter-service restaurant. We offer tasty, nutritious meals with a free-will pricing model for our guests. Our mission is simple—to provide community and healthy meals to all individuals, regardless of their ability to pay.

The Quiltmaker Café's mission is guided by the seven primary elements of the One World Everybody Eats model for café operation:

1. *Social enterprise.* We believe that trust is fundamental in building a community. Organizations prioritizing social goals over profits foster trust within their communities.

2. *Pay what you can at our café.* There is no suggested pricing. Diners are welcome to contribute what they can afford, whether in terms of money or time. Prosperous communities support and celebrate every member, regardless of their means.

3. *Guests choose their portions.* Empowerment through choice is key. Guests specify what they want and how much of each item they desire. This not only empowers individuals but also reduces food waste.

4. *Everyone is welcome.* Food holds the power to unite people. Sharing a meal fosters healthy communities, which in turn contributes to a better world for all.

5. *Space for community.* We believe in a community-led approach to food security. A strong, engaged community is vital for our organization's long-term success.
6. *Opportunity to volunteer.* Our philosophy is centered on offering a hand-up, not a handout. We encourage community engagement through volunteering, fostering a respect for food and its preparation.
7. *Excellent food.* Access to healthy and nutritious food is a basic right. Strong local partnerships enable us to provide high-quality meals and contribute to the strength of our community.

For more information, please visit the Quiltmaker Café Website: www.thequiltmakercafe.org

PO Box 852, Pittsboro, NC
info@thequiltmakercafe.org

Printed in the United States
by Baker & Taylor Publisher Services